POCKET ROCKET

PUBLISHED BY

NEMESIS PUBLISHING

62 BALLACRIY PARK, COLBY, ISLE OF MAN, IM9 4LX

ISBN 978-0-9564092-2-5

PRINTED BY:
ANTHONY ROWE, ENGLAND

COVER PHOTOGRAPHY BY GRAHAM WATSON

STEVE JOUGHIN OUTSPRINTS STUART COLES TO WIN STAGE 3 OF THE 1987
KELLOGG'S PRO TOUR OF BRITAIN IN BIRMINGHAM

ALL OTHER PHOTOGRAPHS BY PAUL J WRIGHT

POCKET ROCKET

The autobiography
of
Steve Joughin

with Richard Allen

JAMES BERRY FUND

James was a talented young rider and tipped by many to follow the successes of fellow Manxmen Mark Cavendish, Jonny Bellis and Peter Kennaugh. He was just thirteen-years-old when he died in December 2005.

James was on a training ride in the Isle of Man and died after being struck by a wheel which came loose from a lorry. When Steve asked for a percentage of the proceeds from this book to go towards the James Berry Fund, we were only too happy to accommodate his wish.

The Fund helps talented young Isle of Man cyclists gain experience racing in Europe and is a lasting memorial to James, operating on similar lines to the Dave Rayner Fund in the UK.

In buying this book, you're helping honour James' memory and helping support young Manx riders make a name for themsleves. Thank you for your support.

John Quirk
Nemesis Publishing

CONTENTS

FOREWORD

As a television commentator, there is nothing more exciting than to call the finish of a cycle race where perhaps 200 riders jostle for position; shoulders and elbows clashing as pedals against spokes send out their own messages. Only one can win, and win they must at all costs. These remarkable men race inside their own cocoon, oblivious to those around them; they sense only the magnetic pull of the finish line that they can see as clearly as a hawk about to pounce on its prey.

Sprinters can never win the Tour de France, as the mountains are too high and the stages against the clock too far, but in their own environment, where fast-twitch fibres, fearless skills and strong desires combine, they are unbeatable. When I look at a television picture of a fast-finishing bunch of riders, what I say next is not scripted. Like the sprinter, my words are a reaction to a situation, so I thank Steve Joughin for crediting me with his well-earned nickname, The Pocket Rocket. Exploding out of the pack, this little bundle of energy from the Isle of Man - where the national flag has three legs and the cats no tails - was so often the highlight to my day at work.

Steve's 21st century contemporary, Mark Cavendish, will forever more be known as the Manx Missile, a title which I thought fitting because once launched he never veers from his line as he goes on to win. But when the Pocket Rocket was tearing up the Tarmac, Mark wasn't even born, and it was Steve Joughin who Britain relied on to break up the dominance, especially in the British Milk Race, of the Europeans from (at the time) both

East and West.

This is a long overdue book of a little man with an amazing heart, and a pair of legs that left nothing to the imagination once the chequered flag was raised. Well done to Richard Allen for helping Steve fill a big gap in our sport's great history and for remembering another Manxman in teenager James Berry, who died in 2005 while training to become perhaps the next Steve Joughin.

Phil Liggett MBE
September 2010

PROLOGUE

I was the Isle of Man's answer to Bart Simpson. Or maybe it was Dennis the Menace; my haircut as a kid was more like the latter than the former. But what I had in common with both of them was that, as a kid, every minute of every day was spent thinking up more ways to annoy people and get into trouble on the estate where I grew up.

From this less than promising start I managed to build a career in a sport that came to shape my life. Cycling is a hard sport. Stage races are among the most physically demanding of professional sports, not just in terms of the demands of the races themselves but because of the dedication and hard work required to train week after week, month after month, year after year.

Cycling in Britain has tended to be considered as a minority sport; it has never achieved the status it has in continental Europe where cycling stars rival, and sometimes eclipse, the big stars in football and motorsport. I was lucky in that being born in the Isle of Man meant I grew up in a place that, in terms of cycling at least, had more of an affinity with the sport's heartlands in France or Belgium than it did with the football-mad UK.

This is the story of how I found a passion for a sport that changed my life for the better. It led me away from a childhood that, despite the best intentions of my parents, was leading me towards the wrong side of the tracks. Cycling has given me so much, so many good mates and so many good memories. When I raced in the 1980s and 1990s cycling in Britain was going through a bit of a golden age as it began to emerge from the shadows of mainstream sport.

I'm 51 now and run a cycle clothing company. I still ride, but racing is confined to past masters events and reliving races gone by with other ex-pros. There is a camaraderie in cycling that means whenever ex-riders meet up they end up talking for hours about the races they won, or should have won, all those years ago. Just talking about the races in which we competed makes our legs ache these days. So by the time I've finished this book I'll be more knackered than when I was racing! But there are lots of stories to tell and I hope they will entertain you over the following pages.

After retiring as a professional rider, I missed the buzz of racing. I missed the adrenaline rush of sprinting for the line, the thrill of crossing it with my arms in the air and hearing the crowd roar. It was all gone, forever, and I needed something to replace it. Drinking became the only way I could replicate that feeling, but in trying to find something else to give me the same thrill that racing gave me, I almost lost everything that mattered in my life. There were times when I wanted to end it all. Yet things are much better today, thanks to Alcoholics Anonymous and the support of my wife, Joanne, my two sons and lots of good friends. I've managed to get my life under control and now work as a volunteer for AA to help others with drink problems.

I hope this book entertains you with stories from when I was racing. But I also hope it offers encouragement to others who have had, or continue to have, problems with alcohol.

I wouldn't have achieved what I did in cycling without support and encouragement from my parents. I'm glad they were able to see me achieve the success I had in the sport. Sadly, my mum passed away a few months before this book was published. Mum played a massive part in my life; I inherited from her the mental strength which is so important in a sport such as cycling. Her no-nonsense approach to life has always helped me to stay focused on what I had to do to make it.

I miss her every day that passes.

Steve Joughin
September 2010

Racing for Moducel in front of a huge crowd in the 1984 Douglas Criterium in the Isle of Man

STAGE 1

Idyllic childhood to teenage terror

My school report as a kid could have been summed up with the words: Steve Joughin - good at getting into trouble. I wasn't interested in school and was never going to be an academic. There weren't any sports that I really excelled at either. But I always had a natural instinct for getting into scrapes and causing a nuisance.

Yeah, I was really good at that. And what's more, I enjoyed it. Looking back, it's difficult to work out why I got into so much trouble. I came from a loving home with a mum and dad who did their best for me and my two younger sisters. It was a good home and I was brought up to have good values, so it's difficult to identify why I was such a tearaway. I never set out to hurt anyone, but I damaged property, broke into buildings and generally did anything that would cause annoyance. It's funny how your attitude changes as you get older, because if I saw a kid today doing what I did back then I'd say they deserve a clip round the ear.

I was born in June 1959 in Douglas, the capital of the Isle of Man. Capital sounds grand, but really it's just a small town. The Isle of Man is a tiny island in the middle of the Irish Sea and just thirty-three miles long and thirteen miles wide. It's a Crown Dependency, so although it has the British Queen as its head of state, it has its own parliament and makes its own laws. I grew up in a place that was pretty much idyllic for any kid. The Island is a beautiful place, with mountains and valleys, a stunning coastline and lots of places for kids to run around in. There was virtually no crime, so it was safe enough for parents to let their kids out to play all day if they wanted. I say 'virtually' no crime; I think whatever crime there was at that time was largely down to me and a few mates.

I was a terrible child. I smashed windows, broke into the local roller-skating rink and raced around it at midnight, and swapped numbered garden gates in a whole street so the postman delivered all the letters to the wrong addresses the next morning. Or I would sleep out in a tent in the back garden and wait until the early hours of the morning to play practical jokes on the neighbours; many families in our street used to leave washing on the line overnight in the summer, so a good trick was to sneak over the garden fences and swap all the clothes over from one line to another.

Every troublemaker has an accomplice and mine was Stuart Kelly. He shared my eagerness to make mischief and between us we caused mayhem on the Willaston estate where we spent most of our childhood. We'd play a game called 'black rabbit' - that's knocking on all the doors in one street and running off round the corner as everyone in the street came out to see who was there. As we got older me and my mates became known as the Willaston Shop Boys because we spent a lot of our time hanging around a local store; we haunted Willaston like poltergeists.

As well as causing trouble in the Isle of Man I had an international opportunity to cause mayhem. On a school trip to Ostend the school sent all the kids go-karting but I ended up racing one of the karts through the streets and having a whale of a time until I crashed into a couple of parked cars. I got arrested for that one.

By far the worst trick I used to play was getting a huge dog turd and placing it on someone's doorstep. I would pour lighter fuel on it and set it alight before knocking on the door. The trick was then to hide somewhere that allowed a good view of the house owner answering the door; they would often open the door in their slippers, expecting to see the milkman collecting his cash for the week or maybe the man from the football pools. When they saw their doorstep on fire they instinctively stamped out the flames. Stuey and I would laugh our socks off as we watched another hopping mad neighbour curse the air as another pair of slippers was ruined. I loved the smell of burning slippers in the evening. It smelled of......victory! A cruel trick to say the least, but at the time us kids thought it was hilarious.

While some of my stunts could be written off as high spirits or practical jokes, things became more serious as time went on. My parents, both law-abiding citizens who worked hard to bring their kids up properly, were understandably distraught and couldn't understand why their son was such a bad lad. I couldn't understand it either, and struggle to find a reason even now. Maybe being smaller than the other kids made me want to stand out more and get attention any way I could; I knew I couldn't get it through academic achievement and, apart from winning a school diving championship, I hadn't found a sport or hobby that I'd stuck at long enough to become good.

I often wonder what would have happened to me if I had stayed on the wrong side of the tracks. If I'd carried on my trouble-making past my sixteenth birthday I would have been liable to get the birch, a form of flogging that was still a legal punishment for offenders in the Isle of Man at that time.

One thing I don't regret doing as a kid is playing tricks on bullies. I've never been able to stand bullying of any kind and being small made me a target, but I wasn't going to put up with it. We used to make our own trolleys out of bits of wood and old pram wheels that we'd ride down any steep hill we could find. One day this lad was pushing me around trying to steal my trolley. Eventually, he got hold of it and jumped on it to ride down the hill. He thought he'd got the better of me but just before he rolled away I put a lit cigarette up the back of his school jumper so that by the time he'd got to the bottom of the hill his shirt was on fire. That I don't regret, but the tricks I played on the innocent citizens of Willaston I do regret.

Luckily for me, and for my neighbours, I found cycling. And it was my nose for nuisance that led me to the sport that would change my life. I had seen cycle races before as the Island had a week-long international event that attracted some of the world's top riders. Over the years Eddy Merckx, Tom Simpson and Barry Hoban and other big stars had raced in the Isle of Man, but I'd never taken much interest in cycling up until that point. The TT races were what inspired me back then. I wanted to emulate the TT greats, such as Mike Hailwood and Giacomo Agostini, who raced motorbikes around the Mountain Course, a thirty-seven and three quarter-mile road circuit that was closed to allow racing to take place. The TT is still going today and riders average more than 130mph, but even when I was kid they were clocking tremendous speeds and risking their lives to pursue their passion for victory.

The Mountain Course is also used for cycle racing and I'd ridden it, aged ten, on my old bike. It took me eight hours to complete; I was missing from home for so long that a search party was sent out. I would never have guessed at the time that twelve years later I would lap the same course in under ninety minutes and become the first cyclist ever to ride the course at an average speed of more than 25mph. But apart from that circuit as a ten-year-old, and whizzing around the estate on my old bike, I'd never thought that much about cycling as a sport.

One day, a gang of us went to watch a race during the Manx International Cycling Week. To be honest, I was only interested in flicking stones into the wheels of the riders as they passed. I loved the pinging sound they made as the little pebbles bounced off the spokes. Yet for some reason, that day stands out. I was thrilled by the speed of the riders as they flashed by; the multi-coloured jerseys and the gleaming, lightweight bikes. Something about the race struck me as really exciting. And if it was exciting to watch, I wondered what it must be like to be part of a race, speeding down steep hills and fighting elbow to elbow with the other riders.

For a kid who loved the buzz and excitement of doing dangerous things, this sport was perfect. I already had a friend who was into bike racing and it was to Eddie Kewley that I turned to in order to find out more. I went to watch Eddie race, but don't remember that much about the event, other than I had to sit in the back of Eddie's dad's Morris Mini van sharing the space with a sheep that Eddie's dad had won in a darts match.

But I was determined that I wanted to be a racer rather than a spectator and over the next few weeks my life began to change. The late nights spent plotting devious schemes to annoy the residents of Willaston gave way to early nights in bed so that I could recover from the training I'd done on the bike. It's a cliché to say that sport changed a person's life and prevented them from a life of crime. But some clichés are

17

true, and I do believe that discovering cycling changed my life for the better.

I was fourteen and riding my bike every minute I could, and I met a guy called Geoff Quine, who was to become a big influence on my cycling career and my life. Geoff persuaded me to ride a race for kids held at King George V Park in Douglas. I didn't have proper cycling kit at this stage so turned up in jeans and trainers. I got a red hot poker and burned a groove in the sole of my trainers to that they would slot onto the pedals and make it more like riding in proper cycling shoes. I got dropped in the race but wasn't put off. I met a few lads who I joined for training rides and all of the work I was putting in started to pay off. After just a few weeks of training, I finished second in a 21-mile handicap race.

On the back of this performance I decided that I deserved a proper racing bike and started to pester my parents to buy me one. I can understand why they weren't keen because they had become used to me taking up sports and hobbies only to get bored with them after a few weeks. But this time it was different. I had a part-time job at a butcher's shop and started to save my own money. Eventually, I had enough to buy my first proper racing bike and became the proud owner of a Jennsen 'Pratt Special'. My mates said it was an appropriate name.

The bike was two inches too big for me and I was doubled up on the seat as I stretched to reach the handlebars when I rode it. But despite that, the bike became my pride and joy and, like many kids before and since, I polished it until you could see your face in it. There were no stainless spokes or carbon rims back then so I polished the chrome rims and spokes with Duraglit to keep them gleaming.

By 1974 I was approaching my fifteenth birthday and getting ready to leave school. I joined the Manx Road Club, which has produced many champions over the years. Current pro riders Mark Cavendish, Jonny Bellis and Peter Kennaugh are Manx Road Club riders, as are Great Britain Olympic Academy riders Mark Christian, Tim Kennaugh and Chris Whorrall. When I joined the club it allowed me to develop even more as a rider, although some old habits were difficult to shake off. It seems daft to think about now, but, while I was piling up the miles in training, I was still smoking. On club runs we'd stop at a café for a bite to eat and while the other lads were inside tucking into beans on toast, I'd be outside having a fag. Smoking and trying to become a pro bike rider don't really mix and my mum pointed that out one day. She asked me what I wanted to do with my life and I confidently replied: 'I want to be a pro bike rider.' Quick as a flash she bent down and whipped out a packet of fags that I'd hidden down my sock. 'Then you'll have to give up these things, won't you?' she said.

Despite smoking in my early days I was making good progress and in 1975 I became club champion. I put in some good performances in time-trials, but my real strength was in sprinting. Right from the start of my racing career I felt that I had something that few other riders could match. It wasn't something I specifically trained to improve, just something natural I had deep down in the fast-twitch muscle fibres. As a teenager I was not much more that five feet tall and usually one of the smallest guys in the race. The other riders just couldn't believe that I could generate so much power.

I felt that I had talent as a rider and had made my name in races in the Isle of Man. But to continue my progress I would have to race more in England. I also had to face up to leaving school and getting a job, and I got a place as an apprentice diesel engine mechanic working on lorries and buses. But even after I gained my qualification, I knew that I didn't want to spend my life crawling on the floor under engines. The thought of that just made me more determined to forge a successful career as a cyclist.

STAGE 2
Junior Champion

By 1976 I had a coach, an ex-road racer from the Isle of Man called Ron Killey. He was a great help but there were times when I didn't agree with all of his decisions. For example, that year he wouldn't let me ride the Peter Buckley series in the UK. It was a season-long series for junior riders named after the Manxman who had won the Commonwealth Games road race in 1966 but was tragically killed in a racing accident aged just twenty-five. The series continues to this day and even though Pete's name is no longer used in the official title it is still referred to as the 'Pete Buckley series' by many riders.

I was young and eager to race so it was frustrating that Ron wouldn't let me ride the series. I thought I could do well. So instead I put more effort into training and fitted as much as I could around my job as a mechanic. Getting a friend, usually Ron Killey or Mike Kelly, to ride a Honda 90cc motorbike so I could train behind it was something I tried to do a lot in order to improve my speed.

The rest of the time was spent training with the Manx Road Club. We would often train with riders from other clubs which meant riding with crazy characters such as Loll Jones, who rode for the Ellan Vannin Cycling Club. Like me, he had a taste for winding people up and doing anything for a laugh. He had a rare talent for being able to fart on demand. These days he'd probably be on Britain's Got Talent but back then his unique gift could only be used to entertain his mates.

Loll seemed to have a different job every week. But whatever he was being paid to do in order pay the bills his real passion was always cycling. He was a practical joker but sometimes we turned the tables on him. Once he came out of a café after a break during a training ride to find his bike had been dropped over a 30mph road sign. Another time someone put a load of fireworks in his saddle bags which blew them to bits. You'd think episodes like that might put him off cycling for life, but he took it all in his stride and the last I heard he was still cycling and working in a bike shop in Majorca.

In cycling you come across many riders who have a passion and enthusiasm for the sport. But those who go on to do it for a living have to have more of those qualities than the rest. As a teenager, I saw a lot of riders of my generation who started off with the same enthusiasm as I had but as time progressed many dropped out of the sport. You would hear that they'd got a car or a girlfriend and had suddenly packed in racing. I was the same as most other lads at that age but, regardless of whatever else was happening in my life, I still wanted to race. In the winter, when the weather was too bad to ride, I'd walk round the house like a bear with a sore head due to the frustration of knowing that I'd missed a day's training.

One of my main rivals when I began racing was a Manx lad called Peter Gage. He was a real powerhouse and as good a sprinter as me, if not better. Work and marriage meant that Peter gave up the sport in his younger days. He is in his fifties now and racing again at club level in the Island, where he is a familiar and popular figure. I think Peter was good enough to become a pro, but cycling is a young man's game and if you are going to make a career out of it you only get one chance.

Cycling at elite level is so demanding that riders often

have to make stark choices early in their adult life. It means sacrificing training for another career and missing out on a lot of the social life most teenagers have. But the rewards are great, and it is only by giving the sport your complete focus that you can hope to make it to the top. I did miss out on many things as a teenager, but it was worth it when I won races.

Cycling was to give me so many memories that will stay with me all my life and even as a teenager I was getting a great deal of satisfaction from the sport. One of the most pleasing things when I started winning races was seeing how proud my parents were when my name or photograph appeared in the local newspaper. I'd given them a hard time when I was a kid, yet despite me bringing them so much grief whenever I got into trouble, they had always tried to support me in whatever I wanted to do.

In 1976 I began to pick up some results that would bring my name to the attention of the cycling press beyond the shores of the Island. That was the year I beat a talented young Irishman called Stephen Roche, who just five years later would win Paris-Nice in his debut season as a professional with the Peugeot team. In 1987 he would win the three biggest races in the world by capturing the Tour de France, Tour of Italy and World Road Race Championship. I raced against Roche twice in 1976 and beat him in a junior time-trial and in the Onchan Cup Road Race in the Isle of Man. My good form continued with a second place in the Circuit of Ashurst, after which I headed for the Mersey Division Junior Road Race Championship.

By now my ability as a road sprinter was becoming well-known on the junior racing scene and I knew that I would be a marked man in the Mersey Division race. As a cyclist, diet and nutrition are important factors in racing; a rider burns so much energy during racing and training that replacing that energy is vitally important. However, despite what modern sports scientists might say about pre-race nutrition, it is possible to win races despite not having the ideal diet and without the benefit of all the energy bars, whey protein powders and the like that riders use today.

Before the Mersey Division Championships I knew I was one of the favourites to win and was incredibly nervous on the morning of the race. I forced myself to eat a cooked breakfast, but when I arrived on the start line I felt sick and threw it all up. Not the ideal preparation. I was facing a 50-mile road race on an empty stomach. Yet I managed to win, and proved that sometimes you don't have to be too particular about cramming in thousands of calories before a race of that distance. The Mersey Division win was my biggest so far and the greatest achievement of my career to that point. I must have worn the champions' jersey for a week after that race.

Racing in the UK was now part of the normal routine. At that time the only real option to get to races in the UK (or 'across', as we say in the Island) was to take the ferry to Liverpool. For junior riders in the UK a trip to a race might mean a car journey early on a Sunday morning but for Manx riders it meant a whole weekend getting to and from a race. Travelling on the ferry certainly toughens you up. Nowadays, there's no smoking on board but back then the ferries would be full of smoke and when the sea was rough you would have the smell and sound of people throwing up, and hear cups and plates smashing as they were thrown around the canteen as the boat pitched in the waves. Even when the weather was gale force I'd sit on deck underneath my cycling rain cape just so I could breathe fresh air. Strangely, there

Winning the Merseyside Junior Championship near Ormskirk in 1977

were benefits of having to go through this to get to every race in the UK. Having to make that journey made me that much more determined to give my best when I got there. It paid off that same year with victory in a national junior series, sponsored by the Liverpool Echo, and a ninth place in the British National Hill-climb Championship on the climb of Horseshoe Pass near Llangollen.

I was starting to discover that I had a real talent for the sport; not just the physical ability to win races, but the mental ability too. I hadn't been any good at academic subjects at school but one thing I could do was focus my mind on thinking about a race and getting mentally prepared to push myself to the limit when needed.

Today, top cyclists have sports psychologists to help them 'get into the zone' but a lot of riders don't need anyone to help them do this – they just do it naturally. It's interesting to read in Mark Cavendish's autobiography, *Boy Racer*, when he talks about the time the British cycling team sent him to see a sports psychologist, and how he felt that he gained little from it.

Many of the techniques taught by psychologists are things that just come naturally to some people and that's how I felt about my mental preparations for a race. I was able to focus on my own performance and on what I needed to do to get the best out of myself. When it all came together, I went into races feeling that no matter what anyone else did, I was going to win. That's a quality that Cav has in abundance and is a must-have for a road sprinter. We may both be sprinters, and hail from the Isle of Man, but I would never think of comparing myself with Cav. He has qualities that most bike riders can only dream of possessing.

When it came to dealing with defeat while racing as a teenager, there was no point making excuses if I lost a race; my mum was ruthless and she could always see straight through any excuses I made. That was no bad thing as it meant that whenever I lost I was always looking ahead to how I could put things right in the next race.

By 1977 my confidence was high as I entered my last season as a junior. I won a big race at the Eastway circuit in London in a junior race that was put on in support of a professional event featuring the legendary Eddy Merckx. For British cycling fans, having Merckx race in Britain was like a visit from the Pope. The crowds were huge, and a lot of press were there, so winning the junior race was a good way of getting noticed, even if it was overshadowed by the main event. After I got the great man to autograph a programme for me, I put on a real show, winning five of the six primes before winning the race itself. It was a big win, as all the top juniors were there, including Dave Akam and Pete Longbottom, who would both go on to successes at senior level, with Akam going on to ride as a pro.

I was still riding for the Manx Road Club and that year my main aim was to win the British National Junior Road Race, which just happened to be in the Isle of Man and on a course which came within a few yards of my home. Racing in front of all my family, friends and club mates added to the pressure, as did the knowledge that I would be the favourite considering my good form and the fact that I was racing on roads which I knew like the back of my hand.

It proved to be one of those golden days when everything clicked. Today they would say I was 'in the zone'. Everything seemed right. I was confident and, as if to illustrate that feeling, I wore my Merseyside regional champion's jersey instead of my Manx Road Club kit. I felt completely calm and had one of those days when I seemed to have a heightened sense of myself and my surroundings. 'It will take one hell of a rider to beat me today,' I thought as I climbed onto my bike.

If there was one man who could beat me it was Russell Williams, who was a good track rider and would turn pro in the 1980s. At the time Russell had a bit of a reputation as being a 'wheel sucker', that's a rider who is reluctant to ride at the front of the bunch and share the pace. Russell would let other riders make the pace so that he could save energy, meaning he would have more left when it came down to the sprint. As the old joke goes, there was more work in a doctor's note. Wheel sucking, or 'sitting in', is a tactic of racing; all riders do it from time to time but if you get a reputation for doing it more often than others, it goes against one of cycling's many unwritten rules. Wheel sucking in cycling is equivalent to the footballer who dives to get a free-kick or penalty. It's not against the rules as such, but it's generally frowned upon – especially if someone does it to you and you end up losing as a result.

The junior championship was a hectic race right from the gun. It was a hilly course and there were strong winds; a typical race on Manx roads. Attacks were going left, right and centre, but through all the mayhem one thing remained constant; every time I looked behind me I saw Williams right on my wheel. As we went into the last of the fifteen laps there was a lead group of thirty riders, half the number that had started.

When it came to the sprint I decided to go from a long way out, and got the jump on Williams and the other guys. I'd won the national title, and in my home town too. I stood on the top step of the podium as they played the Manx national anthem, Land of our Birth, and thought this would be the only time I would ever be lucky enough to win a national title on home soil.

There's an old saying in sport that you are only as good as your last game or last race. I found that out after winning the national junior title, as I went from a tremendous high to an even bigger low. My national win gained me a place in the British team for the World Championships in Austria. It was a great opportunity, but it turned out to be a disaster, for myself and the British team. None of us finished, and I crashed out on a rain-soaked course that made the event more like a scene from the chariot race in Ben Hur than a bike race. I even managed to ruin a barbecue for a few fans as I ploughed into the grill they'd set up at the side of the road. I sent plates and food flying everywhere. To make things worse, they didn't even offer me a burger when I'd picked myself up off the floor.

Winning the Willaston Handicap in 1977

The British press loves nothing more than building up a team's chances only to kick them when they are down after a disappointing performance. The GB team's track squad didn't fare any better, so we all trooped back home to read press reports which branded us all as failures. Just for good measure, our team manager Tom Pinnington decided to lay into us as well, saying we lacked guts. One weekend I was a hero in the Isle of Man and felt like I was on top of the world, the next I was written off as a no hoper.

I knew that if I was ever going to make it as a pro rider I had to get over disappointments quickly. So instead of moping about the disaster in Vienna, I looked ahead to the Peter Buckley junior series which I was leading with just a couple of races remaining. A victory in the Peak Forest leg of the series increased my lead and all I had to do was put in a decent performance in the final race to become the first Manx rider to win the series.

Before that final event I had to tackle the Tour of Ireland, not against other juniors, but mixing it with continental professional riders and senior amateurs. In the field was Pat McQuaid, who won the Tour's prologue and was a good rider. He's now the president of the UCI, the world governing body of cycling. I think I was the first 18-year-old ever to ride this tour and it felt daunting to think that I would be up against much stronger and more experienced riders. Not only that, but the race distance was a lot further than I'd been doing in junior events. The Tour of Ireland was a nine-stage race averaging 100 miles per day. And that was 100 miles over tough terrain. Ireland is a beautiful country, with its green pastures and rolling hills. But if you're on a bike it can be brutal. The climbs are hard and the roads are what bike riders call 'heavy'. That means the kind of road surface that's rough and doesn't allow bike wheels to roll as much as they do on smooth Tarmac. We also used to joke about some of the roads being dual 'cabbageways' because many of them had grass and other vegetation growing up the middle. Put all this together, and add in wind and rain, and it is enough to make any race in Ireland tough.

However, being from the Isle of Man, which has a strong Celtic influence and similar terrain, it meant Ireland was a kind of home from home and I was racing with the Island team, alongside my old mates Loll Jones, Mark Gage and Eddie Kewley. On the eve of the opening prologue time-trial in Cork the four of us were nervous, as we knew the next nine days would make for some epic racing. The prologue was a one-mile race against the clock up St Patrick's Hill in the centre of Cork. It's a twenty-five per cent gradient that has been the scene of some great races over the years. It was used in the Nissan International Classic in the 1980s and featured in the Tour of Ireland as recently as 2008. Short time-trials often suit sprinters and I knew I could put in a decent ride, but didn't know if it would be good enough to be competitive against experienced pros. So I was delighted when I crossed the line to finish sixth.

It was a great start for me but the next day was a different story, as we set off to race 100 miles or so from Cork to Kenmare. I needed everything to go right for me, so I was fuming when I had a problem with my bike early on in the stage. The bike was not handling properly; there was an issue with the headset and I went back to the team car three times to get it fixed, but it still wasn't right. Finally, out of pure frustration, I stopped and flung the bike into a hedge. The forks on the bike snapped, which was kind of lucky because it showed there was a major problem with the bike, and if I had carried on the forks could have snapped while I was riding. Twenty miles into the tour and my race appeared to be over as the team didn't have a spare bike to fit me.

I climbed into the team car and sat there cursing my bad luck until one of the race organisers, Morris Foster, pulled up in his car and offered me a bike that was small enough for me to ride. I got on and fought hard to catch the peloton. A breakaway had already gone clear and would stay away all day. But I was in the main bunch as we came into Kenmare to find out that it had been market day and thousands of cows had been herded along the finishing straight. The cattle had gone by the time we got there but they had left behind lots of presents for us and the road was now a river of runny cow shit. Everyone in the bunch got covered in it as it sprayed up off the wheels. It had been a crap day in more ways than one but I won the bunch sprint and that lifted my spirits for the rest of the race.

Two days later there was a 125-mile stage finishing in Limerick, the longest of the race. I was starting to feel the fatigue from having to race day after day, over distances far greater than I had experienced as a junior. I got dropped on the road to Limerick and sat in what is known in cycling as 'the laughing group' or 'autobus'; the group of riders at the back of the race who aim just to finish a stage within a time limit and so avoid disqualification. On hilly or mountainous stages it's where you will usually find most of the sprinters, although you won't find many of them laughing on the really hard stages. But on this day there was genuine laughter as we rolled along telling jokes and just enjoying being on the bike. We had a lot of laughs in that race, including watching some of the race officials dashing out of the pub just as the bunch arrived in town and then hurriedly writing down race numbers as they sprinted for the line in intermediate hot spot sprints.

Racing in Ireland had a character all of its own and the rules were a little less harshly enforced. So when I felt my strength returning I decided to leave the laughing group and attempt to get back up to the main bunch. A big lorry went past us carrying a load of hay and I sprinted after it and sat behind the truck nicely tucked into its slipstream and sheltered from the wind. Mark Gage was with me and we stayed behind the truck until we saw a car up ahead towing a caravan and our other Isle of Man team mate, Loll Jones, tucked in behind it. We caught the bunch with about ten miles to go and I was first over the line in the bunch sprint again.

The way we'd pegged back the bunch by getting a tow behind vehicles wasn't strictly within the rules. We even got a hand-sling from the chief commissaire as he drove past!

But as I had not been in contention to win the stage, the race officials and most of the other riders didn't mind. I was a young rider trying to find my feet in a big senior race for the first time. They were prepared to turn a blind eye as they recognised I was just trying to survive. But not everyone saw it like that; my Island teammate John Purvis thought I should have been disqualified and tried to stir up some trouble for me. I felt that there was a bit of jealousy, that I was starting to make a name for myself; and in a small place like the Isle of Man, that meant I was getting more headlines than other Manx riders who were also ambitious.

In response, I just got my head down and won another bunch sprint on stage seven, and even though it was tough, I was somehow surviving each day and felt that I was getting stronger with every stage. By the time we got to the finish in Dublin I was starting to feel that I could make a living at this game. The last stage was a circuit race around Phoenix Park. I took third place on the stage and finished the tour in 15th place, about ten minutes behind the Spanish pro Angel Arroyo who would go on to win stages of the Tour de France and the Tour of Spain in the 1980s.

Many pro riders will tell you that riding a tough stage race produces a period of top form in the following weeks. It's as though your body is over-compensating for all of the suffering you have put it through day after day. I returned from Ireland really flying and won the final event in the Peter Buckley junior series by attacking alone in the Raleigh-Wentworth 60-mile race, a victory that also clinched the series.

I was chuffed to bits and felt that the idea of turning pro some day was now a real possibility rather than just a dream. At that time I felt I was too young and was prepared to go back to work at a nine-to-five job for a few years before getting a pro contract. But at the end of 1977 I was offered pro terms by Falcon team manager Billy Holmes. I was astonished that a top UK outfit would want to sign an eighteen-year-old with hardly any experience of senior racing, but Billy was waving £1,800 under my nose, which was a lot of cash to an apprentice mechanic.

At first I wanted to snatch Billy's hand off, but Ron Killey advised me to wait until at least after the 1978 Commonwealth Games, and that's what I did. Today, it's possible for riders to race as professionals and still compete in the Commonwealth Games and Olympics. But back then I had to make a choice; remain as an amateur and go to the Commonwealths, or turn pro and turn my back on any future Commonwealth or Olympic involvement.

I decided that I wanted to represent the Island in Edmonton, and Ron said it would be best if I finished my motor mechanic's apprenticeship so that I would have a trade to fall back on if I couldn't make a living from cycling. So at the end of 1977 I went back to the garage, where most of my work mates were now taking an interest in what I achieved on the bike and most of them respected what I was doing.

Some of the bus drivers didn't share that respect; they seemed to look down on us mechanics and thought we were something that they wiped off the bottom of their boots. They obviously thought that a five-foot two-inch-tall teenager covered in oil was someone they could treat like dirt and get away with it. They obviously didn't know me very well. I remember one driver who was a real big-head and used to like to order me about. Now, kippers are part of the Isle of Man's staple diet and have been for centuries. I don't know whether this driver liked them or not, but even if he did, he would have got fed up with smelling them all day; I strapped a couple of kippers to the exhaust system which used to get nice and hot as soon as the engine was running, so he and his passengers had long days of the bus stinking of fish. As 1978 approached I was getting ready for a full season of racing as a senior. But there was, and always would be, a bit of that impish little kid in me.

STAGE 3
The DHSS performance plan

Britain is currently a world-leading nation in cycling and the success story that led to the current generation of world beaters began in the 1990s with the setting up of the World Class Performance Plan (WCPP). It was the brainchild of Peter Keen, the man who had coached Chris Boardman to gold at the Barcelona Olympics. The WCPP used the latest thinking in sports science and aimed to make the most of the cycling talent Britain had by analysing every detail and using the expertise of coaches, nutritionists and psychologists. The accumulation of marginal gains is how the coaches describe it. Whatever fancy terms they attach to it, the system works.

The WCPP was to lead to the current Olympic Academy and Olympic Podium programmes for elite riders, programmes that produced Mark Cavendish, Bradley Wiggins, Chris Hoy, Victoria Pendleton and most of the other British stars who have achieved success on road and track in recent years.

I think it's great that British riders now have access to such support and don't begrudge them any help they can get if it assists them in winning at world level. But it makes me smile when I think back to what it was like for myself and other young riders when I entered the senior ranks in the late seventies.

We didn't have a World Class Performance Plan – we had what I called the 'DHSS Performance Plan'. At a time when there was mass unemployment in the UK, myself and many other riders signed on the dole at the DHSS (Department of Health and Social Security) and claimed unemployment benefit in order to be able to pay the bills while we trained in the hope of getting a pro contract. For me, it seemed the only chance I had of getting out of a dead-end life.

I didn't sign on the dole until the end of 1978, a season which would include the Commonwealth Games in Edmonton. The winter of 1977/78 had gone well, although it was hard for me to find the time to train after a hard day's work in the garage. That often meant doing 40 miles in the dark on my own, or a shorter, faster session behind a motorbike. For the motor-paced sessions I relied on Mike Kelly and Ron Killey, who gave up their own to time to help me and it is the kind of support that I appreciate to this day. The hard work paid off and the season began well with a victory on home soil. I then picked up a fourth place in both the Eddie Soens Handicap and the Circuit of Ashurst, two races in the UK which meant long ferry journeys.

I had raced in the UK as a junior and got used to four or five-hour ferry trips and long road journeys to get to races. When money was really tight, I would play hide and seek on boats bound for England and stowaway on board to save paying the fare. I had a part-time job with a fruit and veg firm and every now and again had to drive a van full of Manx kippers onto the boat going to England. If I had a race in England coming up, I'd hide my bike and kit bag in the back of the van. When I went to the port, I was supposed to drive the van onto the ferry and leave the keys in the van for the driver in Liverpool to collect. I used to do all that, but instead of going back ashore, I would hide in the toilet until the ferry left port and then get my bike and kit bag out of the van and head off to race. As I say, times were hard and I had to resort to that sort of game in order to be able to get to the races I needed to be in if I was to make progress.

It helped to have friends in Merseyside offer me lifts and my old mate Frank Daniels was a big help in this regard. He regularly used to pick me up at the docks and drive me to and from races. That kind of help meant a lot to me at the time, and still does. Having to make a trip by sea and road to get to a race may be seen as an obstacle to riders from the Isle of Man. But if you are prepared to make the journey, I think it makes a rider race that much harder when they get there. Why go all that way just to give up when it really starts to hurt in the last few miles of a race? My mate Mike Doyle now coaches the Island's national team and he says those long ferry journeys are good for building team spirit. Certainly, the current generation of Manx riders who are producing world class performances have not been held back by having to cross the Irish Sea so often to race in England.

Peter Kennaugh, the talented Manx rider who is now a pro with Team Sky, had to race a lot in the UK in order to further his career. He not only had to sacrifice his own time to race but his parents had to spend a lot of time and money to support him in his ambitions. Pete says that he didn't keep going all the way to the UK in order just to finish in the top ten. He went there to win, and he did just that, with a successful career as a junior which earned him a place on the British Cycling Olympic Academy, which then led to a pro contract. That attitude of drawing extra motivation from having to make more of an effort to get to big races is something that I recognise from when I was racing.

People often ask about why a place the size of the Isle of Man has always produced good riders. That question has cropped up more often in recent years, with Mark Cavendish leading the current generation of international riders from the Island. But the Isle of Man has always had a regular stream of good riders going back to Peter Buckley and pro riders Nigel Dean and Mike Doyle, both of whom I raced with during my career. There are many factors making the Isle of Man a good breeding ground for cyclists, from the ideal terrain and relatively quiet roads to the Manx International Week, which helped create a cycling culture and raised awareness of the sport among kids. From the 1930s up until 2003, when Manx International Week came to an end, the Isle of Man attracted some of the world's greatest riders to race. Tour de France champions Eddy Merckx, Jacques Anquetil, Laurent Fignon and Stephen Roche all raced in the Island. Add to that list the names of Tom Simpson, Rudy Altig, Sean Kelly, Robert Millar and Barry Hoban - to name but a few of the stars who raced in International Week - and you get an idea of the quality of racing that was right on the doorstep of any kid growing up in the Island. Seeing such superstars competing on Manx soil certainly had an effect of inspiring many kids to take up the sport. Another factor in the creation of the Island's cycling culture.

But at grass roots level too there were unique aspects of racing in the Isle of Man that helped create talented riders. It was, and still is, normal for junior riders to race with seniors. This was because there often weren't enough riders to have separate races for juniors, so as a kid I would ride 40-mile handicap races against riders of all ages and all abilities. I believe this type of racing helped me progress more quickly and was something that gave Isle of Man riders an advantage over junior riders in the UK, who would be riding their own separate races with riders of the same age. Race organisers weren't as bothered about rules and regulations as they were in the UK; in the Island, it was very much an attitude of getting stuck in and having a go, and it's still the same to a large extent. In the Island, it's all about getting bums on bike seats.

In the UK there are historical reasons why time-trialling became the big focus and overshadowed road racing for many years. But in the Island, massed start road racing was always the focus and this, combined with the fact that the Island's hilly terrain made it ideal for road racing, is another important factor. The weather in the Isle of Man is often cold, windy and misty – although when the sun shines it is one of the most beautiful places in the world to ride a bike. The bad weather means that you have to be determined and passionate about cycling, and it means Manx riders are used to the cold and wet, which was useful for me in the 1978 Girvan Three-Day race in Scotland. I felt like I was suffering with hypothermia for most of the race because it was so cold, but managed to finish fifth in the criterium stage, which was held in driving snow. During the Girvan, when I wasn't freezing cold, I felt as if my legs were on fire due to a strong embrocation called Capsulin which I used during that race. Out in the cold it was okay, but as soon as you stopped and came indoors it felt as though someone had set fire to your legs. It was like Napalm, and was made worse if you had a bath or shower. It was so thick that you had to use a mixture of lemon juice and washing-up liquid to get it off your skin.

The burning sensation from using Capsulin had just about worn off by the time I arrived in Northern Ireland a few weeks later to ride the Half-Way House Grand Prix. It was raced on a big circuit and I crashed on the first of nine laps but got up and managed to get back in the bunch. With two laps to go

I attacked and went clear with Stephen Roche. Stephen was a regular visitor to the Isle of Man as a junior so I knew him well. I had beaten him before, so felt confident I could do so again. On the final lap we were still together and I just rode him off my wheel to win by forty-five seconds and take my first victory as a senior.

Looking back at that race, it seems remarkable that Stephen went on to win the Tour de France, Giro d'Italia and World Road Race Championship all in the same year; Stephen was a good rider, but at that time I would never have dreamed that he would win what he did. If I'd thought he was that good I probably wouldn't have attacked him!

During 1978 I raced against, and finished ahead of, two other riders starting their senior careers and who would go on to become big stars in continental racing; Phil Anderson, who in 1981 would become the first Australian to wear the leader's yellow jersey in the Tour de France, was one and the other Robert Millar, the Scot who finished fourth in the Tour de France in 1984 and won the King of the Mountains jersey.

After the Half-Way House I returned for a race in the Isle of Man, the Fred Kelly Memorial, which I won. Then it was back to Northern Ireland for the Tour of Armagh. At this time The Troubles featured on the news almost every night and the late 1970s was a particularly violent period. In 1979, a year after I was racing in the Tour of Armagh, the IRA killed eighteen members of the Parachute Regiment at Warrenpoint in Northern Ireland and on the same day killed Lord Mountbatten in the Republic. In all the years of The Troubles, the IRA attack at Warrenpoint was the highest death toll suffered by the British Army in a single day. The county of Armagh was considered to be one of the most dangerous areas; British soldiers on duty in Northern Ireland used to refer to parts of Armagh as 'bandit country'. It was a nervous time to be riding a bike race on open roads and there were often stories about the convoy of race vehicles being used to smuggle guns if the race crossed the border between north and south. Some people said that whenever a race crossed the border, the convoy would get a little bit longer. In the Tour of Armagh I won the second stage by out-sprinting the local star, Billy Kerr. At the end of each stage we would all gather in the hotel bar for a drink and I remember looking around and wondering if some of the guys in there were members of the IRA. But I always loved racing in Ireland and found it difficult to connect the wonderful people I met there with the horrific acts of violence I saw on TV or read about in newspapers.

After Armagh I finished second in the Merseyside Divisional Championship and went into Manx International Week with a lot of talk in the Island about me winning the Manx International senior race at my first attempt. I wasn't confident, as I was still getting used to racing as a senior and would be up against an England international team that would be tough to beat. But the week started well, with a third in the Mountain Time-Trial in a time that was then the fastest ever by a Manxman – 1hr 35m 47s. I then won the Willaston Handicap, which was on the doorstep of where I grew up, and again finished ahead of Roche.

Things were looking good for the Manx International, but three days before the race I crashed in the Douglas Kermesse and ended up semi-conscious in the road lying in a pool of blood. The crash looked worse than it was, but I needed stitches in my face and I'd picked up a few bruises. I spent the next day - the day before my nineteenth birthday – in bed. When the Manx International came round I was on the start line and things went much better than I expected. The race was decided by a two-man breakaway of Steve Lawrence and Robert Millar, and they finished in that order. The race, held over a circuit which included the tough climb up to Snaefell Mountain, brought Millar a lot of attention and alerted many in the sport to his tremendous climbing ability. In fact, two races in the Isle of Man bookended Millar's career; his last ride as a professional was his victory in the Manx International in 1995, which was also the British Road Race Championship. I finished tenth in the 1978 Manx International, two minutes behind Millar. The next weekend, I was in Preston for the Leyland GP and broke away with John Purvis and won the race in a sprint. Almost a minute behind me was Millar, who would win the British amateur title a week later.

As part of my build up to the Commonwealth Games I rode the Scottish Milk Race with the Great Britain team and then it was off to Edmonton. I went into the road race with some commentators considering me as a possible winner. The race was fast, with Millar and Phil Anderson setting the pace. I attacked from the bunch in an effort to catch the break but crashed and punctured my rear tyre with just twenty miles remaining to the finish. By the time the team car had reached me with a new wheel, the race was over. Anderson won and I finished eight minutes down. I'd given up a chance to turn pro in order to go to the Commonwealth Games and I knew this may be my last chance of a medal, as once I did turn pro I'd no longer be eligible. I was devastated that I would be going home empty-handed and in moments like that it feels as though you have no future and no hope. It's as though your whole world has collapsed. Yet by the time I arrived home, I'd started to get over it and my mood was helped when I beat Anderson and Roche in the opening prologue time-trial in the Tour of Ireland and won the stage. I slipped down the general classification as the race went on, but it was a good win for a 19-year-old against some top class riders.

At the end of 1978 I met the great road sprinter Barry Hoban, who at the time had a British record of eight Tour de France stage wins. His record was only beaten when Mark Cavendish passed his total in the 2009 Tour and he marked the occasion by sending Cav a bottle of champagne. Barry was a top sprinter in the late 1960s and early 1970s and, as well as winning stages of the Tour de France, won Ghent Wevelgem, which makes him one of the few British riders to win a classic on the Continent. Barry gave me some sound advice about sprinting and I picked up some good tips on tactics and on how to get in the right frame of mind to win sprints. Barry was, and is, a typical Yorkshireman and tells things as he sees them. He used to tell me that sprinters who said they lost a race because they got boxed in were just making excuses. He told me that a sprinter must get in the right position in the bunch a few miles from the line, not just in the final few hundred metres. Good sprinters never let themselves get boxed in. It was good advice and I listened and learned from a man who had ridden against, and beaten, some real legends of cycling. A few years later, Barry left the continental circuit and raced a bit in the UK and I ended up beating him. After one race I'd won he came to me and said: 'That's it Joughin, I'm not helping you anymore!' But I appreciated the advice that Barry had given me and learned a lot from talking to him and racing against him.

As winter approached in 1978, I completed my mechanic's apprenticeship and when I left the garage on my final day I promised myself that it would be the last time I ever spent eight hours a day getting oily and dirty under a bus or truck.

I moved to Liverpool where, ironically, I would spend the winter living in a converted garage. At that time Liverpool was the strongest region in Britain in terms of cycling talent. I would often train with the Liverpool Century club, which would have a chain gang of up to sixty riders. I signed on the dole and claimed unemployment benefit which allowed me to train virtually full-time. At the time there were a lot of UK riders doing this. Some people said it was wrong, because it gave us an advantage over amateurs who were working. They called us 'secret professionals'. But I had no qualms about it. I was only doing what the so-called 'amateur' riders did in Eastern Europe. They were all supposed to have full-time jobs in the military but all they did was ride the bike and trained like pros. It's no wonder the Russians dominated events such as the Milk Race for so many years. The Brits who tried to compete weren't just taking on a team of Russian cyclists, they were going into battle against the Red Army. And the British Cycling Federation sent them into battle without any guns or bullets. Some of us decided that if we were going to be competitive against the Eastern Bloc teams, then we'd have to train full-time just as they did; but even if we trained full-time we would still be at a disadvantage because the Soviets and East Germans had support from the best coaches and sports doctors. Of course, we now know that some of the sports doctors were giving many of the Eastern Bloc riders something a little more potent than aspirin.

I decided to make the best of the situation I was in and that meant signing on the dole and training full-time. At a time of mass unemployment in the UK there were few jobs around anyway, and for me cycling seemed the only way I could improve my life, so I wanted to give myself the best chance I could of getting a pro contract. I knew that it was no longer possible for a rider to stick strictly to the amateur ideal of holding down a full-time job and training part-time, not if you wanted to compete with the best. Those people who criticised me, and others, for signing on and training full-time were living in the past and clinging to the image of comic book sportsmen such as Alf 'Tough of the Track' Tupper, who would work all week in a factory then, fuelled by fish and chips and brown ale, beat all comers in running races. The days of Corinthian ideals were long gone and, looking back, me and the other amateurs who became 'secret professionals' were actually ahead of our time.

Within a few years the distinction between amateurs and professionals would be abolished, with pro competitors being allowed to compete in the Olympics, and in the 1990s British Cycling would set up its Olympic Academy and Olympic Podium programmes using National Lottery money to fund full-time riders as they trained for the Olympics and World Championships. No one working full-time and training part-time would have a hope in hell of winning an Olympic or World Championship medal today. It is accepted by all coaches that to be the best requires complete focus and dedication to that goal. That's the accepted wisdom now, but a few of us had realised that thirty years ago.

Today's talented British riders are paid a lot more than we received on the dole all those years ago, and the British Cycling programme gives riders the best advice in training and the best equipment, which riders deserve and need if they are to compete on a level playing field with the rest of the world. But essentially it's an extension of what we were doing – talented young riders being funded by the state to allow them to make the most of their ability. In the 1980s we were doing it off our own bat and were not sanctioned by the powers that be. British Cycling may now have fancy titles for its development programmes, but I like to think that it's really the DHSS Performance Plan by another name and there are more skin suits to go round in today's GB team. We had to share them and hand them over to someone else once we'd finished our race!

In 1979 I was in Liverpool with my mate John Purvis and the fact that two Manx riders had moved to the UK a year or so before the Moscow Olympics was enough for newspapers in the Island to start speculating about us getting a place in the team. In fact, it was true that this was part of our plan but reading about it in the press added a bit of pressure and I suddenly realised the magnitude of what I was aiming to do. I was still just a talented young rider. I had potential, but to get a seat on the plane to Moscow meant I had a season and bit to prove that I was among the best in Britain. The only way I could convince team selectors, and to an extent myself, that I was good enough to go to the Games was to compete in the season-long Pernod-sponsored British road race series.

I needed a good season with consistent results, but it didn't start well. In the Essex Trophy in March I'd only done about twenty miles when there was a crash right in front of me. Instinct takes over in moments like that and I automatically swerved to avoid the rider in the road and luckily there was no hedge or wall at the side of the road, so I ended up riding across a garden. The next thing I remember is being underwater; I'd plunged into a lake after riding down a steep embankment. It was freezing cold and a shock to the system after being warmed up from racing. I floundered in the water for a few seconds as my life flashed before my eyes. I eventually found the bike, but had to dive down six feet to get it. It was Harry Hall, the famous bike shop owner and team mechanic, who pulled me out and I headed straight for the team car and sat there shaking. It's a funny story to tell now but at the time it scared the life out of me. One of the strangest experiences I've ever had as a cyclist – or, for that matter, as a swimmer.

While we're on the subject of bizarre happenings in races, I'll tell you about something else, but those of a sensitive disposition may want to skip to the next chapter because it doesn't make for pleasant reading. Whenever you speak to people who don't understand cycling they often ask how riders go to the toilet during races. For pro riders it's not easy, as the race will not wait for you while you make a call of nature. Often riders will take the chance to make a 'pee stop' when there is a lull in the race or sometimes riders will take a pee while riding along and being pushed by a team mate. It happens in big stage races but riders are supposed to do it away from areas where there are lots of spectators and can be fined by race officials if they don't. But what if you want to do more than pee? This is where it becomes more of a problem.

There's a story Paul Kimmage tells in his book, *A Rough Ride*, about the 1989 Tour de France when he saw Greg Lemond, who won the race that year, riding in front of him during a stage in the final week of the race. Kimmage thought that Lemond had a particularly good suntan on his legs that day but as he got closer he noticed an unholy smell. Yes, you guessed it, Lemond's legs weren't brown because of the sun but because he'd got a bad bout of diarrhoea and couldn't risk stopping to go to the toilet, as it was a crucial stage and he didn't want to lose time.

I was in a race once and saw a similar thing. I won't say where, or who the guilty party was, but this is what happened. During the race there was a breakaway up the

Liverpool Mercury Crits, August 1980

road. I was in the peloton and there was a lull in the racing as we rode down a narrow lane. I saw a rider in the bunch taking his jersey off and just thought he was changing it. After removing his jersey he then began to pull his shorts down and everyone started laughing because we all thought he was just going to do a moonie, but he had something else in mind – he slid his backside off the back of the saddle and proceeded to take a dump right onto the back wheel of his bike. If you've got an earthy sense of humour it sounds funny, doesn't it? But the wheel of a racing bike spinning at hundreds of revs a minute acts like a farmer's muck spreader. Suddenly all of this crap was being sprayed over all the riders behind him and the peloton parted like the Red Sea as everyone tried to avoid being showered in human fertiliser. Because we were riding down a narrow lane, there wasn't much room to manoeuvre so several riders got splattered – and I'm glad to say the perpetrator of the muck-spreading ended up with a nice mucky line all the way up his back. The next few miles were spent with riders telling him what they thought of him while showering him with water from drinks bottles. A strange tale from the peloton, but there were some even stranger times ahead.

STAGE 4
War of the wheels

I had enough money left to keep me over the winter and began to think of my plans for 1980, an Olympic year. Those plans began in 1979 and as the season approached I already had some major targets set for the months ahead. Top of the list was the Manx International which, after the British National Road Race Championship, was the most coveted prize in UK amateur cycling. Being from the Isle of Man meant the Manx International was even more important to me.

I hadn't been feeling great as Manx Week approached; I'd had a cough and my best racing bike had been stolen in Liverpool. I was due to ride a few other races before the week culminated with the big one. I decided to ride the other races, but to save as much energy as I could and keep my powder dry for the International.

The big day arrived and the weather was typical for the Isle of Man – gusty winds and rain. The main obstacles to me winning were the England team and a strong mix of riders from across Europe. There was also Stephen Roche again, who was now becoming known as one of the best amateur riders in the world. I was riding in the colours of the Manx Road Club but I was carrying the hopes of the Isle of Man, and certainly felt a bit of pressure; I knew I was capable of winning and that many people in the Island were expecting me to win.

The race was held over three laps of the TT motorcycle race course which meant three ascents to the top of Snaefell Mountain. I managed to get in a decisive break with some of the more experienced internationals, although I hadn't really contributed much to the group and tried to save energy by sitting at the back of the pack. That seemed fair to me as I was only a 19-year-old kid in a group of more experienced riders. But even though I had tried to save energy, I was on my knees on that final climb. In all the times I had ridden up Snaefell, that day was the worst experience I'd ever had.

Roche was chasing us and was closing rapidly, so there was no let up in the pace on the climb. I was yo-yoing off the back of the group, losing ground then desperately clawing my way back to the leading riders. The gradient of the climbed eased off towards the summit and I was able to hang on as we began the descent to the finish in front of the TT Grandstand; but it was still eyeballs out as we rode hard into a strong headwind.

We came into the last half mile, which was dead straight, and I could see the Grandstand in the distance. I was tucked at the back of the group and waited as a couple of the guys feinted as if they were starting their sprint. I let them play games until the sprint started for real. The breakaway group broke ranks and I saw daylight ahead. In that instant the sprinter's instinct takes over. Suddenly, I saw nothing but the gap between two riders. It's like having tunnel vision; in that moment I was aware of nothing but firing myself towards the finish line. In a split second the race was over. I could feel that I was leaving everyone else behind. Five yards from the line I knew I'd got it and threw my arms in the air in a victory salute. It made a good photo in the papers, but could have been a lot different as a gust of wind almost blew me off my bike. I managed to stay upright and was mobbed by friends and family as soon as I had crossed the line. It was a perfect day and it all seemed like a dream. The Manx International was a big race in its own right, but for a Manxman it was an extra special occasion.

Somehow I managed to get out of the crowds around me and I climbed onto the podium and held the trophy aloft. That prompted the biggest roar that I'd ever heard. I wasn't the only one there that day that thought they had been dreaming. My former PE teacher, Don Beard, emerged from the crowd to congratulate me. No doubt he remembered me as a kid, never having much interest in school and always getting into trouble. I suppose I can't blame him being surprised that I had achieved something with my life. 'Joughin,' he said to me, tears of joy running down his cheeks. 'I just can't believe that you have done this.' And then, just to emphasise his point, he added: 'I can't believe that YOU have done this.'

The headline in the Manx Star newspaper read: 'Joughin's Crowning Glory' and it carried a report by my old friend Geoff Quine, who wrote a great piece saying how he was in tears at the end of the race because he felt so proud to be a Manxman. Things like that stay with you forever; it's the kind of moment that motivates you to make all the sacrifices you have to make to be a success in a sport as tough as cycling. That day was one of the greatest moments in my life and the next day was my 20th birthday. Before you ask, yes, I had a bit of a party that night.

After the Manx International, I was below par at the British championships and it meant that I was unlikely to get a place in the team heading for the Moscow Olympics the following year. Jim Hendry at the British Cycling Federation, the sport's governing body in the UK, had already said enough to make me believe that I wasn't going to be in the team so I wasn't surprised when I didn't get a ticket for the plane to the USSR. Instead, I was given a ticket to somewhere far more exotic, and a lot more dangerous.

A harpoon gun is not something you expect to see in the back of your team car when you are about to start a bike race. Spare wheels, drinks bottles and rain capes, yes. A good team manager should always be prepared for anything that can happen during a race - but was he expecting an attack by Moby Dick or Jaws? Being at a big international stage race was a new experience for me, so I was ready to expect the unexpected. But I'd grown up on a quiet Island in the middle of the Irish Sea, so when I arrived at the Tour of New Caledonia it all came as a bit of a shock. To be honest I'd never heard of the place.

The adventure began a month earlier when I got a call from Jim Hendry. I thought he was winding me up when he mentioned the Tour of New Caledonia.

'If you think I want a bloody ten-day tour of Scotland in October you're out of your mind,' I said, demonstrating that I should have paid more attention in geography when I was at school.

'It's not Scotland,' said Jim. 'It's an island in the South Pacific, a French colony. The government there is throwing big money at the race. Teams from France, Italy and Switzerland are going and there's a huge prize list. I'm doing you a big favour by bringing you on it.'

As Jim filled me in with the details I started to get excited by the idea. It was 1979, I was 20-years-old and had won the Manx International race a few months earlier, my biggest win so far. The UK season was coming to an end and I hadn't got much to look forward to. I was living in a smart converted garage in Liverpool but was having to scratch around for part-time work to tide me over for the winter. So once I heard there was a chance of free trip to the sunny South Pacific, and the chance to earn some big money, I leapt at it.

I'd never been any further than Belgium at that time so it was going to be a big adventure; what I didn't realise was that we were going into a war zone. I travelled to New Caledonia with another British rider, John Dowling from Hemel Hempstead, who I soon discovered was a good rider and a good guy to race with. It seemed to take forever to get there and we arrived worn out even before the racing began. We had a week to acclimatise, though, and needed it to get used to the intense heat and humidity, not to mention the snakes, bats, lizards and giant insects. We had already been told that some of the first Europeans to land on the island were eaten by cannibals, so we were a bit nervous to say the least. The French had used the island as a penal colony at one point so this added to our nervousness as the race approached. Who was it who once described pro cyclists as 'the convicts of the road?'

Anyway, as I was getting ready for the first stage of the tour I was putting on my crash hat when I looked into the back of the team car, which was actually a pick-up truck, and saw the harpoon gun sitting next to a pistol and the usual collection of wheels and bottles. I turned to our team manager, Jean-Pierre, and said; 'What's the spear gun for? Are you going shark fishing after the race?'

Jean-Pierre looked around as if to check whether anyone else was listening. Then, in a low voice straight out of an episode of *Allo' Allo'*, he said: 'Leesen, Steeve, whatever 'appens on ze road, you don't stop. Just keep going, I'll be behind you and if ze Kanaks come out of ze jungle at you, I shoot zem and I have to make sure zey are dead.'

Jean-Pierre then jumped into the car and I cycled off to the start line in a daze wondering what on earth I had got myself into. Here I was, a bike rider from a tiny but peaceful island and suddenly I was in fear of being attacked by jungle tribes. I later learned that the Kanaks were the indigenous population and there was a guerilla war going on against the French colonialists. At one stage France declared a state of emergency and sent paratroopers. As luck would have it, my natural ability for finding trouble had struck again, only this time my sixth sense for mayhem had surpassed itself by landing me right in the middle of a revolution. So I rolled off to start a ten-day stage race through mountains and jungle, where it seemed that dropping off the back of the bunch might be very bad for your health. There are many phrases in cycling to describe being dropped from the main group of riders. One is 'being hit by the man with the hammer'. It was a metaphor that might just come true in the Tour of New Caledonia, I thought. And the man might be armed with something worse than a hammer. Because the race organisers were expecting trouble, all of the team managers had cars that were tooled up like an SAS battalion in case the Kanaks decided to attack the race to get publicity for their cause.

New Caledonia only had one major town – Noumea – and only one surfaced road, so most of the race was on dirt tracks. The island is about 250 miles long and about 30 miles wide and down the centre is a ridge of mountains, with some of the summits as high as 5,000 feet; equal to some mountain passes in the Tour de France. Being a French colony meant that there was a cycling culture on the island and it was a beautiful place to ride, even if you did feel the need to keep your head down.

As it turned out we didn't get ambushed by any guerrillas

but it was a hard race on dusty roads that were so bad that those following in cars were all wrapped up under masks and bandanas to protect themselves from the dust being thrown up. We had to ride in temperatures of up to 100 Fahrenheit and the race was like a scene from the Tour de France from before the war, with riders on dusty roads and some of us riding along with big leaves under our cycling caps to try and keep cool. Also, similar to the Tour in the old days, the time gaps in New Caledonia were huge due to the number of punctures and crashes. On one stage a rider may be virtual leader on the road and the next day he could lose twenty minutes. Yet most of the riders were happy because the prize money was so good and it went from first to last place. There were other bonuses, too, such as being given coconut milk by locals who cracked them open with their machetes. There was plenty of fresh fruit, too, and on some stages we were even able to stuff ourselves with roast wild pig. We were treated like conquering heroes in some villages as we cycled over a blanket of flowers strewn across the road. At night we would sleep in the jungle, with the occasional spider or snake for company, and the next day race a hundred odd miles in sweltering heat. It was like the Tour de France crossed with *I'm A Celebrity Get Me Out of Here.*

Considering there were a lot of experienced European riders in the race it was surprising that a local lad from the island won the tour. I finished thirty-first overall, with my mate John Dowling seventeenth. At the time, the fact that I went home with £2,000 in my pocket was more important to me than where I finished in the race. I reckon it was equal to winning around £20,000 today and was more money than I had ever seen.

Back in England I'd been scratching around trying to make

a living but the Tour of New Caledonia had given me the taste of a different life. It wasn't just the food and fruit that felt exotic; I had a taste of life as a professional bike rider and I loved it. After the tour a few of us were invited to ride a track race on the island of Vanuatu, which was also a French colony. I rode really well there and won an omnium event (a series of track races in which riders score points and the rider with the best total score wins) which attracted a lot of attention and won me some more prize money.

There was a six-day track race coming up in Tahiti and there was talk of a contract for me to ride it. A few weeks earlier I was facing a bleak winter in the grey streets of Liverpool but now I was racing in the South Pacific with the sun on my back and plenty of money in my pocket. It was another world compared with the one I'd left behind in England and the Isle of Man. For a while, I even had dreams of staying out in the South Pacific and making a career racing there and in Australia. Then it all went wrong.

After I'd won the criterium, I went windsurfing, something I'd never done before in my life. I got into trouble and was swept out to sea. I swam for miles and somehow managed to get back to the beach dragging the board with me. I'd been out in the open for hours and got sunstroke. My sunburn was so bad I had to spend five days in hospital; I had blisters all over my body and a high temperature. My dream of staying in the South Pacific had been shattered. Suddenly England and the Isle of Man didn't seem so bad and I felt homesick. I flew home with skin falling off me like snow and having to go into the aeroplane toilets to towel myself down to ease the itching as my skin peeled off. I got back to Liverpool and, like any young working class lad with a few quid in his pocket for the first time, I went straight out and bought a car – a Ford

Escort Mark 1.

Looking back, I had been sent to New Caledonia as a kind of consolation and maybe that did me a favour. I'd had a taste of life as a professional bike rider, I'd won a bit of money but also had to deal with getting sick. Ever since cycling had become my passion I had dreamt of being a pro, but dreaming is different to experiencing it for real. In New Caledonia I'd learned some valuable lessons – that there is a lot more to being a pro bike rider than being able to turn the pedals fast and win races. It's as much a test of mental strength as it is of physical fitness. You have to rely on yourself, motivate yourself and have the determination to ride out the tough times. In New Caledonia, when things had gone wrong, my first instinct was to pack my bags and go home. Was I really cut out for living the nomadic life of a professional cyclist? Could I cope with living out of a suitcase for months on end?

At that time I still wasn't sure whether I could cope with it. But I knew that I didn't want to spend the rest of my life crawling around under diesel engines, which is what I had trained to do. At that time I was still really just a kid. I sometimes wonder what would have happened if I hadn't gone out windsurfing that day and hadn't got sunburn. Maybe I would have stayed in the South Pacific and my life would have been completely different. I've never been back to New Caledonia but would love to go one day and revisit the place. In the end, the experience didn't deter me from pursuing my dream, but the road to a professional contract would have a few more twists and turns before it became a reality.

STAGE 5
Men of steel

I was glad to get back home from New Caledonia and had some good news on my return. I received a phone call from Dave Aston who wanted me to join Manchester Wheelers. It had been a cycling club like any other in the UK until a man by the name of Jack Fletcher got involved. He was a cycling nut, but also a successful businessman who owned the Trumanns Steel company.

Officially, clubs were allowed to have a sponsor to cover the costs of buying clothing and bikes and also to pay for travel expenses to races. But Jack spotted that this was a bit of a loophole and started to put more and more money into the club. He knew that for riders to achieve their best they had to train and race full-time, a fact that I knew too. Effectively, Fletcher was building a pro outfit but doing it as covertly as he could so as not to incur the wrath of the blazers at the British Cycling Federation. He wasn't the only one putting money into club cycling – Phil Griffiths was doing something similar at GS Strada – but I don't think anyone in the UK put as much money into a club as Jack did into Manchester Wheelers.

Jack wasn't in it to bring himself glory or notoriety; in fact the rules about sponsorship meant that he needed to remain in the background. These were still the days where sport was split into amateurs and professionals. There were amateurs making money and that was okay as long as the governing body of your sport didn't find out. It was all a bit cloak and dagger because if an amateur was found to have received too much prize money, they could be banned from amateur competition. That meant a life ban from the Olympics and Commonwealth Games which for many, myself included, would have been a devastating blow.

It all seems very strange now when we are used to seeing millionaire athletes, tennis players and swimmers competing in the Olympics. The days of a distinction between the amateur and professional codes belongs to another era but back in the early 1980s it was a serious issue. I could see that sport in general, and cycling in particular, was heading towards an increasingly professional approach even though there was still supposed to be amateur competition. But in that era amateurs such as myself were caught in a kind of limbo between amateurism and professionalism. We knew we had to train like professionals just to be competitive in amateur events, but we couldn't openly earn money or accept sponsorship to fund a professional approach, so we had to make money without it being too obvious to the governing body of the sport.

Jack saw what was going on and sympathised with the position that talented amateur riders were in. He also saw that the British Cycling Federation was doing nothing to help British amateurs, who were expected to compete against Eastern Bloc riders, who everyone knew were allowed to train full-time and prepare like pro riders by their own national federations. All Jack wanted was to use some of his wealth to allow talented riders to realise their full potential. I found Jack to be very approachable and not someone who was overpowering. He was friendly and helpful and was always happy to listen. Over the years I got to know him and his wife, Nora, well and they became good friends of mine and had a very positive influence on my life, which made it all the more of a shock when, twenty years later, Jack took his own life. Like many people in cycling who knew Jack I was shaken by the news, and totally mystified as to why he did it. I don't think anyone ever knew why.

Jack had a significant and very positive impact on British cycling back in the late seventies and early eighties. At a time when the national federation had failed to create any structure that allowed British riders to compete on level terms with other nations, Jack was doing what was needed. It was like a logical extension of the DHSS Performance Plan except that it was privately funded and paid the riders more money. It also produced much greater results, and over a decade Manchester Wheelers' riders dominated UK racing. Just look at some of the riders who turned out in that familiar royal blue jersey with the white and red bands and you get an idea of how big an influence the club, and Jack Fletcher, had on the sport in Britain; Ian Cammish, Chris Boardman, Darryl Webster, John Woodburn, Pete Longbottom, Bob Downs, Des Fretwell, Malcolm Elliott, Deno Davie, Pete Sanders, Allan and Mark Gornall, Jeff and Mike Williams, Mark Bell, Sandy Gilchrist and Paul Curran were all winners with the Wheelers.

Of course, the fact that the Wheelers were attracting so many good riders was resented by some involved in the sport. Just as some criticised me and other amateurs for signing on the dole and training full-time, so some people criticised the Wheelers for creating a two-tier system of amateur riders, who had a day job and trained and raced part-time, and those who rode for the Wheelers and other sponsored clubs who were effectively pro riders. The critics of Jack's approach wanted me and all of the other riders who benefited from being part of Manchester Wheelers to go back to the days of Alf Tupper and the rose-tinted view that British riders could train part-time and still compete with the best in the world. Again, just as with the DHSS Performance Plan, Jack's system was really ahead of its time. Eventually the amateur/pro system would be abolished and even the British Cycling Federation would realise the need for funding riders full-time.

Jack's grand design for Manchester Wheelers began at the dawn of Thatcherism and in many ways his thinking was in line with the ideas emanating from Number 10. Jack believed that it was up to entrepreneurs to solve problems, that it was a waste of time waiting for state institutions to put things right. He saw the need for professionalism and the benefits it could bring – and he had the money to put his ideas into practice. A top football club wouldn't expect its players to work all week and train part-time, so why should a cycling club be any different? So Jack brought in cyclists like a football manager would sign players. This was great for me and the other riders who came to ride for the Wheelers as it gave us the chance we were looking for, a way for us to break into professional racing.

For the existing members of the Wheelers, however, all of this came as a massive culture shock. For years cycling clubs had always drawn members from the town or city in which they were based. All of a sudden riders from across Britain were signing up for Manchester Wheelers and it was these new riders who were getting all the glory and were overshadowing any 'home grown' talent the club had. Decades of tradition had been swept away in a few months and a lot of club members didn't like it one bit. Some of these members left in protest at Jack's revolution. Some stayed and tried to fight against the changes – and in some cases that actually meant fighting. I remember Dave Aston, who had been instrumental in devising the new system and was effectively the team manger, having a fight in a car park with another club member over some club kit that hadn't arrived. Sometimes he had a bit of a short temper, but Dave was a smashing bloke. Tragically he was killed in a car crash a few years ago.

It was when I joined Manchester Wheelers that I began to get some advice from the legendary coach Eddie Soens, who was to cycling what Bill Shankly, the legendary Liverpool manager, was to football. Eddie always said that there are only two types of cyclists – cyclists, and racing cyclists. I was always a racing cyclist. He had a big influence on the careers of many riders, in particular the former TI Raleigh pro and multiple time-trial record breaker Dave Lloyd. I used to call Eddie 'Dave Lloyd's brains' because of the influence he had on Dave's career, and without him he was lost.

Stories about Eddie's strict, no-nonsense approach are legendary. He was a kind of sergeant major character but he knew what he was talking about and gave me good advice about listening to my body and not training hard when in fact I needed to rest. There were times when I'd have a few drinks and feel guilty the next day and train really hard even though I would have been better off sitting at home nursing my hangover. Eddie taught me that there's no point in trying to train a tired body.

Some of his training methods were harsh, but I thrived on them. Sometimes Eddie would have me doing four hours on my own and then an hour's motorpacing with him on a motorbike. He would tell me to do that three times a week on some occasions; there were riders who would give up that sort of regime after one week, but I stuck to it and it really brought me into good form. Although Eddie had a lot of success as a cycling coach, he was also a leading boxing coach and worked with former world light-heavyweight champion John Conteh. Eddie made my dad laugh after I'd been overlooked for the Moscow Olympics by Great Britain coach Jim Hendry. 'He couldn't coach a frog to hop,' joked Eddie. But his comment summed up his view of Jim.

One of the benefits of being with the Wheelers at this time was that we went on winter training camps to Majorca, where many pro riders still train to escape the worst of the weather in northern Europe. The training camps were ideal preparation for the season ahead but they didn't always run smoothly, as quite often riders were trying to prove a point before the actual racing season began. On that first trip to Majorca a guy called Brian Lowe really annoyed me by half-wheeling me all the time. He constantly tried to get his front wheel in front of mine to try and show how good he was. My answer to this was the same as it had been when I was a kid and I decided to slow him down a bit with a little trick. One night I got a track pump and filled it full of water then crept down to where Brian's bike was kept and let the tyres down. Next day he just couldn't work out why his good form had suddenly disappeared overnight as the water I'd pumped into his tyres put an end to his half-wheeling and gave me a bit of peace.

There was always rivalry and friction between riders in that Wheelers team. Maybe the money on offer made it inevitable. I remember one occasion when Jack had asked someone to pay me £1,500 for wins in the 1980 season, but I only received £750. It only came to light when I thanked Jack for the money and had mentioned the figure. Jack was fuming when he found out but things like this were evidence of the divisions within the club. In later years there was open hostility between Manchester Wheelers riders Dave Lloyd and Darryl Webster, who at the time were Britain's best time-triallists.

Despite all this, joining the Wheelers enabled me to make progress and the wins came steadily in 1980. I took a stage win in the Elswick Centennial race from London to Glasgow and out-sprinted Sid Barras and Barry Hoban, who had returned from continental racing to compete in the UK.

After the GP of Essex I did two races in Italy and picked up a bad case of food poisoning at a post-race banquet. The timing couldn't have been worse as there were two Olympic trials coming up, followed by what was to be my debut in the Milk Race. The Milk Race was dubbed the 'Round Britain Race' – essentially it was the only national tour in Britain at that time and the only cycling event in the country which had any real recognition amongst the general public. It was an amateur race, but would become a pro-am event in the mid-1980s.

The Lincoln GP was one of the Olympic trial races and the hot weather the day before must have sweated out of me the last effects of the bug that I had picked up. I was going well and the climb of Yarborough Hill felt easy. Joe Waugh led a breakaway with me, Steve Lawrence, Jeff Williams, Gerry Taylor and John Cavanagh. In all there were a dozen riders in the group, which suited me as when we got to the finale everyone was looking around at each other and we slowed to 15mph. That was perfect for me, because when I jumped I built a big gap very quickly and no one was going to catch me.

A one-day race such as the Lincoln suited me but a two-week

stage race was not something I could be competitive in every day. That year's Milk Race was dominated, as it was for many years, by the team from the Soviet Union. They trained like pros and raced liked pros and after two weeks of brutal racing they had placed riders in the top four places and won most of the stages. No British rider won a stage. The Soviets' domination of the Milk Race added more weight to my argument that part-timers couldn't compete with them. It was my first Milk Race and I felt out of my depth. I took a battering day after day and wondered if I would ever be competitive at that level. But Des Fretwell gave me some encouragement, saying that I would win stages of the Milk Race in twelve months' time if I persevered and trained hard. As it turned out, he was right. But that race was so tough that there were two English riders in the Milk Race that year who took such a hammering that they never raced again. Competing against the Soviets could do that to you.

At that time the Russians were just too strong. The British riders would turn up on bikes that were like bags of nails but, as Milk Race director Phil Liggett said: 'The [Russians'} bikes were well-oiled and the tyres were brand new – and the men who rode those bikes were very tough indeed.'

It would be a few years before the race had a home-grown winner and that would only come when it was opened up to professional teams from the UK. The Russians, though, loved the Milk Race. For them, getting to stay in the best hotels made the race feel like a working holiday and a break from the bleak life they had back home. They won a lot of money in the years they dominated the event but the Soviet regime would not allow them to take any cash home. So the Russian riders would ask to be paid the money they had accrued in the first week on the first rest day of the race. As if to emphasise their dominance, the Russian riders would spend the rest day like holidaymakers on a shopping spree buying the wonderful products of western capitalism that they couldn't buy back home. The race organisers would then help them to get their shopping shipped home. Meanwhile, most of the British riders, including me that year, would spend most of the day in bed recovering from the pummelling we'd been given by the 'Red Machine'.

After the Milk Race that year came Manx International Week which included the British Road Race Championship. I made it into the decisive breakaway but with ten miles left Neil Martin took off and only Steve Lawrence could close the gap. Lawrence won and I came in fourth, thirty seconds behind. It was disappointing to come so close; if I could win the national title anywhere, I would want it to be in the Isle of Man.

I'd received a lot of support from the Island and for years the local papers had talked about the possibility of me going to the Olympic Games. I felt that I'd done enough to gain selection for Moscow in 1980 so I was devastated when the team was announced the day after the British road race and my name was not on the list. It was the biggest disappointment of my career up to that point, and a lot of my friends shared my emotions. To have the team announced while Jim Hendry was in the Isle of Man made it worse for me. How he got off the Island after that without being lynched I'll never know. I just couldn't understand why I was not selected. Admittedly, I had not performed well in the Milk Race which had been an event used to determine the final team selection. But no British rider had covered themselves in glory in the Milk Race and, more to the point, it seemed absurd that a two-week stage race was being used to select a team for the Olympic road race which was a one-day event.

At that time I was leading the season-long Pernod-sponsored competition so I could claim that I was the in-form British rider that year. It seemed to me that Hendry had made his decision before any of the so-called selection races and I didn't figure in his plans. This view was strengthened when Steve Lawrence, the man who had won the British title, was also overlooked for Moscow. Hendry said that Lawrence had shown his form too late. The Olympics were still a month away – you could argue that the selectors should have waited another couple of weeks to decide who should be on the plane to Russia.

I consider Hendry to have been a weak manager who was not prepared to make imaginative decisions. When it came to selection for the individual pursuit, it was a choice between Tony Doyle or Sean Yates. Hendry organised an Olympic trial and Doyle won – but it was Yates who got picked. Where's the logic in that?

I would have loved to have proved a point to Hendry by winning the Manx International but my heart just wasn't in it after the disappointment about the Olympic team. The only thing I got from the build up to the Olympics was that all the riders who had been on the shortlist for Moscow were sent for tests with a Czechoslovakian sports doctor – such physiological tests are commonplace now but were in their infancy back then. The sports doctor put us on a stationary bike and measured our power output and was impressed with my results, saying that if I had been born behind the Iron Curtain I would have been trained to become a champion power lifter.

The Eastern Bloc countries were way ahead of Britain in sports science and in Moscow they dominated the Olympic road race, with the Russian rider who had finished third in the Milk Race, Sergei Sukhoruchenkov, winning the gold. None of the British riders made any impression on the race. Even Stephen Roche, who was still seven years away from winning the Tour de France, finished twenty minutes behind the winner. We now know that the Eastern Bloc nations were not just testing riders to improve performance; there was widespread doping going on which was a factor in their domination of amateur sport. Considering all this, it's likely that I wouldn't have made much of an impact in Moscow even if I had been selected, but I think I deserved to have been given a chance.

The only consolation for me at the end of 1980 was that I won the Pernod competition, which was sealed in the final event in the series – the Tour of the Peak in the Peak District. Going into that race, only John Herety (who is now the team manager of the Rapha-Condor pro team) could beat me in the overall standings. So I kept my eye on him and I was right on his wheel when he crossed the line to finish ninth. It was enough to keep me in the top spot. As part of the prize I got a trip to Paris to receive a £500 cheque alongside the great French champion Bernard Hinault, who at that time had claimed two of the five Tours de France that he would eventually win.

The final act of 1980 was the national hill-climb, which traditionally brings the UK season to a close. That year it was held on the climb of Nick O'Pendle in Lancashire in freezing rain. It was a race of only 1,000 yards but it was an eyeballs-out effort and to me such events are a bit crazy. An all-out effort in the freezing cold makes you breathe so hard it feels like you're inhaling razor blades. Hill-climb specialists tend to be a bit eccentric and that year's event had the bizarre twist of the pre-race favourite Jeff Williams crashing while warming up and breaking his nose. But he still finished second and was only one fifth of a second behind Malcolm Elliott, while I came in fourth.

The season was over and I knew that the next year or so would be critical if I was to achieve my dream of becoming a professional cyclist. I was twenty-one and time was moving on. Riding with Manchester Wheelers, with the backing of all that money from Jack Fletcher, effectively made me a semi-professional. But it wasn't the real deal. Riding events such as the national hill climb made me wonder if it was worth staying to race in the UK as I knew that continental pro teams laughed at the British obsession with such bizarre events, along with 12-hour and 24-hour time-trials and tricycle racing, which are equally eccentric to anyone on the other side of the Channel.

To make it as a pro, it seemed that most British riders had to go and race on the Continent. At the time there was a steady stream of British and Irish riders going to race for sponsored clubs in France with the hope of being spotted and signed up by a big pro team. This was the era when Robert Millar, Sean Yates, Stephen Roche, Graham Jones and Paul Sherwen were racing in France and all would turn pro. Continental racing, traditionally so difficult for English-speaking riders to break in to, was experiencing a cultural revolution; a wave of English-speaking riders were in the process of making a dramatic impact.

Over the following few years the Peugeot team, the biggest and most prestigious French team, became dominated by English speaking riders. Roche, the Britons Millar, Yates and Jones, and Australians Allan Peiper and Phil Anderson, became known as the 'Peugeot Foreign Legion'. John Herety and Jeff Williams, who I had raced against in the 1980 UK season, were also off to Europe to chase the dream of a pro contract. My old mate Mike Doyle was already flying the flag for the Isle of Man with the French club Fontainebleau, which included such talents as Laurent Fignon, who would win the Tour de France in 1983 and 1984. Mike was keen for me to join him and, although I was apprehensive about adapting to life in France, I decided to follow the exodus and give it a go at the start of the 1981 season.

At the time I felt compelled to give continental racing a try, but my heart was never in it. I didn't speak a word of French and it wasn't much fun living hand to mouth. I wouldn't have gone at all if Mike hadn't been there already. We raced in France and Belgium and I managed to win a few races. I even got in a breakaway with Fignon in one race and managed to drop him before riding alone to take the victory. 'L'Envolee de Joughin' was the headline in the paper. I worked out that it meant 'The flight of Joughin' and there was a good photo of me riding alone to victory.

I didn't stay abroad long enough to pick up much of the lingo. Mike Doyle says that we only learnt three phrases when we raced in Belgium and they summed up our lifestyle. The first was the Flemish for 'last lap' – that's useful to know when you're riding your legs off in a Belgian kermesse and you want to know how much longer you have to suffer. The second phrase was 'Sorry, but we can't pay' – sometimes money really was that tight. The third phrase is unrepeatable here. Let's just say it came in useful when two young Manx lads were looking to have fun with Belgian ladies who might want to spend some time with would-be cycling superstars.

After a couple of months I returned to the UK. I had given continental racing a try and, while I had some success, I knew that I wouldn't adapt to a new way of life and wasn't

The pain shows during the 1981 Eddie Soens Handicap at Aintree

prepared to sacrifice seeing my friends and family for nine months every year in the hope of getting a pro contract. Also, I just didn't believe that I would ever get that big contract. These days a British rider racing for a continental team can go home several times a year, but back then you were expected to cut yourself off from wherever you had come from. That was something I wasn't prepared to do. I wasn't alone. Phil Thomas, the Liverpool rider who was to become one of my arch rivals on the UK pro scene, didn't want to make that sacrifice either. Once he was trying to explain to a journalist about how big a sacrifice it was for a British rider to race on the Continent. Thomas ended by asking the reporter: 'How good do you think Bernard Hinault would be if he'd been born in Toxteth?'

It was a good point. If you were born in France, Belgium or Italy the route to becoming a pro cyclist was a lot easier than it was if you were from Britain, Ireland or Australia. A few could make the necessary sacrifices and succeed, but I didn't have the single-minded determination to do that. Guys such as Robert Millar gave up everything. Like many of the English-speaking pros who did make it, he lived in a hovel in Paris with the ACBB club, living on a shoestring, cut off from his family and friends in Scotland. To emphasise how determined he was there's the story of how he gave himself an horrendous haircut so that he would not be tempted to go out to the local disco on a Friday night. Maybe it helped that he was always a bit of a loner, but that lifestyle never suited me. I came back from France with a bagful of excuses, but at least I'd tried. When I look back at some of the guys I beat as an amateur – including Tour de France winners Roche and Fignon – it does make me think that maybe I should have toughed it out in France a bit longer.

On my return home I discovered that I'd been selected for the Sealink International, which began in France. So I went back across The Channel for a stage in Le Touquet before the race resumed with the subsequent stages in England. It was at the Sealink that I met Roy Hodges, one of those larger than life characters you'd think were invented by a playwright had you not met them in person. Roy was a rough diamond, a no-nonsense sort of bloke who was great to be around but he also had a furious temper. Roy was working on the race as a masseur and on the boat back to England I was getting a rub down after the first stage. A couple of kids kept banging on the cabin door and Roy got fed up with the noise. All of a sudden he wrenches open the door, almost pulling it off its hinges. He stands in the doorway glaring at the kids outside and drags one of them in by the scruff of his neck. The kid sees me stretched out on the table and Roy points at me and shouts at the kid: 'Right. You're next for the treatment.' The kid must have thought he'd stumbled into some sort of weird torture chamber. Roy was only joking of course, but it had the desired effect and the kids didn't bang on the door again. Maybe I would have turned out different if Roy had lived on the estate where I caused all that trouble as a kid?

If the lad on the boat thought he'd seen the worst of Roy Hodges he didn't realise how lucky he was. One story tells of a rock band playing in a village hall next door to where Roy lived. It was two in the morning and the music was keeping him awake. So Roy went to the hall and told them it was time to stop. The band told Roy where to go in no uncertain terms and no doubt thought that was the end of the matter. But, so story goes, Roy went home, got his shotgun, loaded it, and then calmly walked back into the village hall, still in his dressing gown, and fired one barrel into each of the band's loudspeakers. He bid them all 'good evening' and went home to get some sleep. Characters such as Roy, and the stories that surround them, help riders pass the time during stage races. Telling a few stories and having a few laughs make stage racing bearable when things are going wrong. But in the Sealink International that year there wasn't much for me to smile about. The Czechs and East Germans cleaned up most of the prizes.

The next big event in 1981 was the Milk Race and with

a strong Eastern Bloc contingent. I wanted to banish the ghosts of the previous year when I had suffered badly but I knew that I was in for the toughest two weeks of the season. A top ten finish in the prologue in Brighton was a good confidence booster going into the first stage from Brighton to Bournemouth. We had a fine British team which included Phil Thomas, Mark Bell, Joe Waugh and Bob Downs - but there was no real organisation for me as a sprinter and potential stage winner. Today, a British team with a sprinter who could win the opening stage and take the race lead with time bonuses would build their race strategy around working to set up the sprinter for the win. But it was different back then and there was no talk of organising a lead out train for me. Bunch sprints were just a free for all, with every man for himself.

As you might expect for a race between two British summer holiday resorts it pelted down with rain all day, although it did brighten up as we neared the end. The finish on Bournemouth seafront was a bunch sprint and just the sort of stage I relished. The only complication was that strong winds during the day had caused waves to crash over onto the promenade, leaving big pools of sea water everywhere. Beneath every pool of water there was about an inch of sand and as you rode through them it was like peddling along the beach. When the peloton came into the finishing straight we had about three quarters of a mile to go. Mark Bell was one of the first to jump and I managed to get his wheel. I wasn't sure whether Mark knew I was right behind him so I shouted to him to move over to let me through. A few seconds later I achieved the ambition that I had held for so many years.

The win was a massive step towards a pro career, even if it was to be another couple of years before I made that move.

Winning the Greater Manchester Police GP, May 1981

The Milk Race was a massive event in Britain and had an international reputation too. Winning a stage was one of the highlights of my career and with the time bonus I got for the stage win I also wore the yellow jersey. Ultimately, any ambition I had for overall victory that year disappeared following two bad crashes. I was wiped out by a Russian rider as we came around a roundabout near the finish of a rain-soaked stage to Coventry and crashed again near the finish of the stage to Landudno, when a rider in front of me hit a parked car and I hit him and ended up landing on the roof. Phil Thomas won both stages. I was still lying fifth overall, with four days to go, when Joe Waugh attacked on a climb during a stage to Harrogate and took three Russians clear with him.

But my stage win made up for any disappointments and showed that British amateurs could compete with the Eastern

Bloc riders if they had the right preparation. That Milk Race turned out to be one of the best for British riders in years, with a total of six stage wins in two weeks of racing. As well as my stage win, Mark Bell and Phil Thomas each won two stages and Joe Waugh won one. I think the performance of the British riders pleased the crowds, but also race organiser Phil Liggett. The Milk Race was Phil's baby; he put in an awful lot of work to make the event successful and he must have been getting fed up with the Russian dominance, so a bit of British success was welcome. I've always had a lot of time for Phil, he's just a smashing bloke and someone who grew up on Merseyside and was a regular visitor to the Isle of Man, so we always had that in common.

In the end the Russians won the Milk Race that year but Britons Bob Downs and Joe Waugh were second and third respectively, and both were within two minutes of the winner. To me it seemed as though Downs and Waugh were riding against each other even though they were both in the GB team. Had they rode as a team, I think we would have had a British winner that year. But Joe had sacrificed his own chances of victory in helping Bill Nickson win in 1976, so maybe he didn't want to do the same thing for Bob. And Bob must have got fed up riding the Milk Race for years and seeing the Russians dominate it most of the time, so getting a chance of glory for himself must have been too much to resist. I can see it from both sides, but I do think their rivalry played into the hands of the Soviets that year. The Eastern Bloc riders may have been hard to beat but I got on well with most of them and in the 1981 Milk Race I got to know the Polish rider Zbigniew Szczepkowksi, who would help me to a much needed win later in the year.

After the Milk Race I put in a good ride at that year's

Mountain Time-Trial in the Isle of Man, becoming the first rider ever to average more than 25mph for the 37.7-mile course. My record was short-lived though, as Dave Lloyd beat me by twenty-two seconds. Darryl Webster, who a few years later would win a stage of the Nissan International Classic in Ireland and turn pro with the Spanish Teka team, was third, finishing four minutes behind myself and Lloyd. Darryl was a great time-triallist and over the next few years would put that skill to good use as he became something of a specialist in long, solo breakaways in road races. That's how he won his stage of the Nissan Classic in 1988. To beat Darryl by four minutes was no mean feat and that Mountain-Time Trial in 1981 was certainly the hardest individual time-trial I have ever ridden. It was five minutes before I could talk after the race. When the Manx International came round a few days later, I couldn't get motivated and maybe I'd given too much in the time-trial, so although the week was eventful I finished Manx Week without a win.

Next up was the Scottish Health Race and the title of the event was ironic because I felt ill for most of it. I won the prologue and took the race lead but then my form dipped and I felt constantly fatigued. After only twenty miles of stage three I was dropped and I ended up so far off the back I did something that I'd never done before and climbed off my bike and sat at the roadside with my head in my hands wondering what was wrong. I ended up thumbing a lift and a group of travellers (we called them gypsies back then) very kindly pulled up in a big van full of furniture. They agreed to give me a lift and I lay sprawled across a sofa as the van tagged on to the end of the race convoy. I was even given tea and cakes while they all listened to my troubles. After about forty miles they had to take a different route to the race convoy, so I got out and flagged down a farmer who took me most of the rest of the way, after which I rode to the finish. Everyone was expecting me to have lost a couple of hours after getting dropped so early in the stage so there was some amazement when I came in just twenty minutes behind the winner. But it didn't make much difference; I felt ill all week and abandoned the race on the final stage. My poor form continued as I failed to finish the William Tell GP in Switzerland, but somehow I found myself in the Great Britain team at the World Road Race Championships held in Prague.

Being welcomed by guards carrying machine guns is never great, and racing behind the Iron Curtain was always a bit grim. Having security fences everywhere didn't help either and after only a few miles I found myself in a group that had taken a wrong turn and ended up on a road blocked by a fence. By the time we had done a U-turn to chase the bunch, the race was over. The only good memory I have of that visit to Prague was meeting by boyhood hero, Freddie Maertens, who won his second world title that year and was in the same hotel as the British team. I still have the T-shirt he signed for me that day.

With a string of poor results, I was desperate for a win. Losing left me feeling down and only a win would lift my spirits. In the Tour of the Peak I felt my good form had returned and initiated two breaks, only to be brought back to the bunch. Then Jeff Williams attacked alone and I missed his move and the chasing group that went after him. I felt I had the form to win, but it looked like I'd missed the boat. Then someone appeared who I remember to this day and am grateful for what he did in that race. Zbigniew Szczepkowski rolled up alongside me and Phil Galloway and proceeded to put the hammer down for a full five miles. Phil and I sat on his wheel and it felt like one of the many motor-paced sessions I used to do behind a motorbike. I saw a group up ahead, the chasers who had now caught Williams. As we closed to within a few yards of the group, my mate Zbigniew was still giving it plenty on the front but turned round to me and shouted at me to go straight past the front group when we caught them. Zbigniew was setting such a fast pace it felt like I was riding behind a motorbike. When we did catch the group in front I was going at least 20mph faster than they were so zoomed past without any of the leaders getting a chance to latch onto my wheel. I had four miles to go but held on to win alone, twenty seconds ahead of second place. It's more than a quarter of a century since Zbigniew did me that good turn but I still remember it and am grateful to him for helping me when I really needed a victory. In cycling you never forget riders who help you in moments such as that. The ProVision cycle clothing company I now run means that I make regular business trips to Poland and I still see Zbigniew now and again when I go there.

After the success in the Tour of the Peak, my 1981 season ended with a disappointing ride in the national hill-climb up Horseshoe Pass near Llangollen. It's a long, gradual climb that should have suited me but the rain at the bottom of the climb turned to snow by the time I got to the top and I finished outside the top ten.

The racing was over for the year, but there was one more surprise in store for me, and a welcome one at that - I was named the Isle of Man Sportsman of the Year. I was surprised that I won the award in a year which wasn't really my best. I think the Milk Race stage win sealed it for me, as it was big news in the Island because the race had a huge profile and received good coverage. A win by a British or Manx rider was rare and wearing the yellow jersey just added to the amount of coverage I received for my stage win. My record-breaking ride in the Mountain Time-Trial may also have been a factor, even if the record didn't stand for long. I was pleased to win the Sportsman of the Year award as it was a sign of recognition and appreciation in my home country. But perhaps it's just as well they didn't hear about my adventures with the gypsies in the Scottish Health Race!

Despite the Milk Race stage win and Tour of the Peak victory I knew that I had been too inconsistent in 1981. When the season came to an end I did a lot of thinking and tried to analyse how and why I'd had a year of such ups and downs. I came to the conclusion that I'd pushed myself too hard, a theory that was certainly backed up by my ride in the Scottish Health Race. I hadn't overtrained, but I'd gone into every race that year desperate to win. I was putting myself under a lot of pressure, which was unnecessary as it just wasn't realistic to win every race; even Merckx didn't win all the time. All season I had been tense and constantly worried about the next race and how I was going to perform. I decided to focus on a few races each year, when I would aim to be in peak form and in between times be more relaxed and not bury myself when I had little chance of victory or when it was a race that wasn't a major target.

This was a better attitude, and in hindsight a more professional and mature approach to the sport. 1982 was a big year, as the season would end with the Commonwealth Games in Brisbane. The Games was a massive event for me as a Manxman because it was the only major international competition at which I could represent the Island. I may have decided to have a more relaxed approach to racing in the season ahead but I still trained as hard as ever. As well as regular group rides and training behind a motorbike, I also did more weight training that winter. When you are sprinting at the end of a race you are using your whole body, so I did weights to develop my upper body as well as leg exercises. Not all bike riders are fans of weight training but I found it really helped. I used to do fifty press-ups before and after every training ride. Malcolm Elliott was another rider of my generation who believed in the benefits of doing weights and he's still doing weights now and still racing. Lance Armstrong is another rider who does a lot of strength training in the off-season.

My training and mental approach was more methodical now and my life had a regular pattern which suited my plans to make the most of the talent I had. I spent winter at home in the Island and got any job I could in order to earn some money and build up some savings to cover me when I was racing in the spring and summer. When the season began in March I would move into a flat in Liverpool, as most of my races were in England and being in Liverpool was handy for getting back to the Isle of Man, with the direct ferry link from Merseyside.

My new regime paid dividends in 1982, as it proved to be my best ever season as an amateur. I was more consistent that year and the season got off to a great start with three wins in a row – the Essex GP, Essex Trophy and Pernod GP. It could have been four wins in a row, but in the Chequers GP, Manchester Wheelers rider Mike Williams got away on his own and there was no way I could chase down a teammate. The Wheelers were now dominating most UK events and we were starting to attract some criticism from other riders and clubs, and in the cycling press, because we had so many of Britain's top riders. But we were just riding races to win and making the most of having a good set of team mates around us.

Winning three races early in the season gave my confidence a massive boost and made all of the effort I'd put in during the winter worthwhile. When I was doing well everything was fine, but it was how I handled defeat that would put my new relaxed approach to racing to the test. That moment came in the Sealink International, which again started on the other side of The Channel, this time in Belgium, including the climb of the Kemmelberg – a twenty-five per cent gradient for a quarter of a mile and with a cobbled road surface. It's regarded as one of the hardest climbs in the spring classics of northern Europe and regularly features in the Ghent-Wevelgem classic. I lost thirteen minutes on that stage – but I wasn't the only one who suffered that day and it didn't bother me. The previous season it was the kind of experience that would have worried me. Instead I saved what energy I could and looked ahead to the next stage in Kent. It was a race from Folkstone to Gravesend and I got away in a break with riders from Denmark, Holland, Belgium and Poland. I was the only Brit in the break and as my GB teammate Malcolm Elliott had the race lead, I was justified in sitting in and not helping to set the pace in the breakaway. By the time we got to the finish, though, there was only me and the Belgian Dirk de Wolf left. De Wolf would go on to a continental pro career, including a stage win in Paris-Nice and a win in the Liege-Bastogne-Liege classic. I beat him easily in the sprint to take my fourth victory of the year, while De Wolf went on to claim the Sealink International that year.

Despite my early season form, and my stage win the previous year, I was not selected for the Milk Race. This confirmed my belief that either Jim Hendry didn't believe in me or he didn't have a clue how to pick a team. As it turned out, I was glad I wasn't picked that year. The Russians dominated the race and filled the top three places, with Mark Bell the only British stage winner. Maybe Hendry had done me a favour by not forcing me to bang my head against the Red Wall for a fortnight.

In Manx International Week I won the Manx Arms Handicap on what was my 23rd birthday; they even played 'Happy Birthday' when I was on the podium. And I was in contention in the final miles of the Manx International, but Joe Waugh was just too strong for me that day. It was a typical Isle of Man day. A Manx myth says that the Island was protected from invaders by the 'Cloak of Manannan' – a shroud of mist which the Celtic god draped over the Island to hide it from hostile forces. Well, the cloak was laid down that day, with wind and rain thrown in for good measure. On the final climb to Snaefell I was in a break with Joe and riding right on his shoulder. Then he changed up a gear but kept the same pedalling cadence, which left me hanging on. I had to dig deep, but managed to ride alongside him and mumble a few words about me not contesting the sprint if he stayed with me to the finish. I don't know whether Joe believed me or not, but he let his legs do the talking. He just fixed his eyes on the top of the climb, shifted up another gear and that was the last I saw of him until the finish.

In the British National Road Race, I was third after my Manchester Wheelers teammates Jeff Williams and Pete Sanders broke clear. After the race Jim Hendry's apparently illogical selection process produced yet another surprise. Williams had won the national title in convincing style – but he was not selected for the World Championships in Goodwood, but Pete and I were picked. Of course I was pleased, but it didn't help me understand how Hendry came to his decisions when picking teams.

In the 1980s there was little for British fans to cheer about at the World Championships and the 1982 Worlds were no different for the men. However, those championships will always be remembered by British cycling fans for Mandy Jones' magnificent gold medal ride. For the men, it was another year of disappointment. All through my career British riders seemed to get worked up about the Worlds, desperately trying to gain selection every year, only for it all to end in an anti-climax as the event passed without any medals for GB riders. When Manxman Jonny Bellis won a bronze in the under-23 road race in 2007, he was the first British man to win a road Worlds medal since Graham Webb took the amateur title in 1967. Les West's fourth place in 1970 was the only real highlight until recent years, with the successes of Jonny and World Championship gold medallist Nicole Cooke.

In 1982, Mandy's gold meant that the British team didn't get quite as much flak as usual from the UK cycling press when the riders returned. By the time the Commonwealth Games came around in October, I had already built up a comfortable lead in the season-long Raleigh Trophy series in the UK and felt confident on the way to Brisbane. I would have Mike Doyle, who would later turn pro, and Mark Gage to support me in the Isle of Man team. We rode the 100km team time-trial, which was a four-man event, but only myself and Doyler ended up doing the lion's share of the work. I suspected that Mark only went to the front when he saw TV cameras. We ended up finishing last, which wasn't a great confidence booster going into the road race a few days later. That ended in disappointment for me, too, as Malcolm Elliott got all the glory sprinting to win gold.

If you go into the newspaper archives and look at press reports about the race you will read that I finished eighth and that I had struggled due to 'stomach cramps'. That was the official reason given for my performance; the real reason was a little more embarrassing – or funny, depending on how you look at it. Any experienced competitor or coach in any sport will tell you that it's a bad idea to use new equipment or clothing on the day of a big event. New kit should be tested before a big race – and that's what I would usually do. For some reason I did a very stupid thing before going to Australia. I bought a new pair of shorts especially for the big race. I decided to go for the best shorts around so that I would have maximum comfort and chose a pair made by Descente, which were the best you could get. The shorts were excellent quality – the only problem was that they were about two sizes too small. I don't know why I decided to ride in them, but I did, and for most of the race all I could think about was the pain of having my balls crushed by these shorts. I was in agony, and I didn't care who was winning after a few hours of racing. As the race went on, the pain spread from my groin up into my torso. I don't know how I finished, but I certainly learned a painful lesson, that's for sure.

There was another strange incident in 1982, when Mike Doyle and I won a load of gas cookers in the Dublin-Galway-Dublin stage race. It was a bizarre prize at the end of bizarre race. I was part of a four-man breakaway coming into the finish of the final stage in Phoenix Park in Dublin and was race leader on the road. With me was Phil Cassidy, who was a great rider, most remembered for twice winning the Ras Tour of Ireland, and Phil would finish second overall if our breakaway stayed clear. Initially the other two guys in the break, Tony Lally and Jamie McGann, didn't want to work with us but Phil and I promised them they could fight out the stage win between them if they worked together and helped us secure our first and second places overall. Lally and McGann agreed and as we got into Phoenix Park they went off to contest the stage win. Or so they thought. We came to a junction and the lead car went left but Lalley and McGann went straight on. Phil turned to me and said: 'They've gone the wrong way, that's last year's route...' So we followed the lead car and entered the finishing straight. As we were sprinting it out for the stage win on one side of the road, we looked up to see Lally and McGann sprinting for the win on the other side of the road but in the opposite direction. I wasn't fussed about taking the stage win as I'd won the race overall, so let Phil take victory. He crossed the line with his arms in the air as Tony Lally came the other way doing the same thing. In the end the commissaires gave Phil the stage win and placed me second, with Lally and McGann given third and fourth place respectively.

My prize for winning the race was a load of gas cookers and Mike Doyle won some gas fires, so we had the problem of getting them all back to our homes in the Isle of Man. The cookers and fires were worth a lot of money, especially when I was struggling to make ends meet at the time. When I finally got one of the cookers back to the Island I discovered that it was only designed to work in Ireland and wouldn't work anywhere else; so much for all that hard work in the race. In the end, a few of the family got gas fires that worked on bottled gas and I had one too. And my mum eventually got a new cooker after we got it converted to work on Manx gas and it's still in her kitchen to this day.

Gas cookers weren't the most bizarre prize I ever won as a cyclist. As a junior I won a race and a load of primes at an event sponsored by a frozen chicken company. At first I thought my mum would be made up with them; no need to go shopping for Sunday dinner for a whole year. So I turned up at Liverpool Airport proudly carrying my prizes and looking forward to presenting my mum with them all when I got back to the Island. I was only a kid and I hadn't thought that Customs might take a dim view of someone trying to import frozen livestock on a passenger flight. The Customs officers wouldn't allow me on the plane and took them off me. I don't know what happened to the chickens, but I suspect it was the Customs officers who ended up having Sunday dinner on me for a few months. One of the Customs men did take pity on me, though, and gave me one chicken to keep. He stuffed it into my kit bag and told me to keep my gob shut as I got on board. So my mum did get one Sunday dinner out of it.

Having to scratch around and make the most of whatever prizes I won summed up my situation at the end of 1982. I was almost running out of options. I'd achieved as much as I could as an amateur and I hadn't been able to put up with the demands of racing on the Continent. Yet I still wanted to turn pro, and I was about to get the chance to do that in Britain.

STAGE 6
Pro rider

There comes a time in everyone's life when they have to make tough decisions which can determine the path their life will take. Mine came late in 1982 when I finally had to make a decision; was I going to attempt to realise my dream of becoming a professional cyclist, or did I just not have the nerve to do it, and would therefore become one of the many talented amateurs who never make it?

I remember coming home from the Commonwealth Games in Australia in October 1982 and feeling down after a disappointing result in the road race. I was thinking hard about how long I could carry on as an amateur. The fire and the passion that I'd had for racing was beginning to fade because I felt there was little more that I could achieve as an amateur. Another factor that was draining my enthusiasm was the constant struggle to make a living. Racing as an amateur meant scratching around to find part-time work when I wasn't getting any income while racing during the spring and summer. Although being part of Manchester Wheelers gave me some cash to cover the cost of racing, it wasn't the same kind of money I could earn as a full-time professional.

I was the top-ranked UK amateur rider in 1982 and yet I was facing another winter of scrimping and saving. It was time to make my talent for cycling into something I could make a living at. But getting a pro contract was difficult if you were not prepared to live abroad. At that time, if you turned pro with a continental team you had to live abroad and there was no chance of having a family life in the UK.

In November 1982 I met Joanne, who was to become my wife; we've been married twenty-five years now and she's supported me through some great times, and some bad ones. We met in the Isle of Man when both of us were working at a supermarket in Douglas. But I had a strong feeling from the beginning of our relationship that we would be together for many years to come and this hope and thought forced me to ask myself some serious questions about where my life was going.

I knew that I was a good cyclist. I'd done enough in the amateur ranks to prove that. I was good enough to win races as a professional. I'd beaten Sid Barras and Barry Hoban in sprints and I was confident I could continue to win races if I turned pro. Cycling was the only real talent I had, but racing as an amateur was like hanging on to part of my childhood. Meeting Joanne and thinking about our future together forced me to grow up. I had to make the move to the pro ranks.

I put the word out that I wanted to turn pro and got a call from Micky Morrison, a guy from Stoke-on-Trent in England who rode for the Moducel team which was based in the city. He said there was a chance of a place for me with Moducel. I was offered a contract, but before I signed I talked to Jack Fletcher, the man who had supported me and many other riders by his funding of Manchester Wheelers. I felt a sense of loyalty towards Jack and his wife and wanted to get Jack's opinion before I signed a pro deal. Jack told me to go for it and in December 1982 I signed a contract with Moducel worth the princely sum of £2,750 per year, plus expenses and

With Great Britain teammates Dudley Hayton, centre, and Sean Yates,
right, before the start of the 1983 World Professional Road Race
Championship in Switzerland

win bonuses. I moved to Stoke-on-Trent with Joanne and we
planned to rent a flat.

When I first moved to Stoke-on-Trent I lived with Micky
Morrison for a month before I found accommodation of my
own. Micky was already riding for the Moducel team and is
well-known to everyone in UK cycling because he is such a
colourful character. It was a rough and ready lifestyle we had
for that short period, like an episode of Men Behaving Badly
about a decade before it was on TV. The only toilet in the
house was downstairs and right at the back. If you needed
the loo in the night you had to walk downstairs, through the
living room and the kitchen to get to the toilet, which was
a real pain. So we got sandwich boxes, which Micky used
to call 'Tiddly Tom Buckets', and put one under each bed
so neither of us had to walk all the way downstairs. We'd

just empty them in the morning. Anything to save time and energy for racing and training.

Micky was always playing tricks. One day we were getting ready for training and my mum came round to visit. Micky was watching daytime TV as my mum sat there talking to me. But on another channel he had a porn video playing. Every time my mum turned to talk to me, Micky would flick the blue movie on and then switch it back to daytime TV when she turned back to look at the screen. All the time Micky was playing it deadpan, knowing that I'd be mortified if my mum looked at the screen at the wrong moment. We had some fantastic laughs together and at that time we were both lucky to have some great riders to train with, which made the miles pass a lot more quickly.

Stoke-on-Trent may not seem the greatest place for pro bike riders to be based but it's in a good location as there are some great training roads on the Staffordshire Moorlands and up to Cheshire Plain. It's really good bike-riding country and in my early years as a pro we had a fantastic group of riders in and around Stoke-on-Trent that would regularly meet and train as a group. John Herety, who rode for Coop-Mercier on the Continent and is now manager of the Rapha Condor team, was there, as was the Aussie Neil Stephens, who would go on to win a stage of the Tour de France and ride for the ONCE and Festina pro teams. And we had Ireland's Martin Earley, who would win a stage of the Tour de France and Giro d'Italia with PDM. Another regular with that training group was Paul Sherwen, who is now known to most cycling fans as co-commentator with Phil Liggett on ITV's Tour de France coverage. Paul has made a good career as a TV pundit, but back in the 1980s when I used to see him on training rides he was one of the best domestiques on the continental scene

Winning the Deeside Spring Road Race in March 1983

with Fiat and later La Redoute. He returned to race in the UK after ending his continental career and won the British pro road title in 1987 while riding for Raleigh-Banana.

After a month or so of sharing a place with Micky Morrison I was looking to move out and find a place of my own. When I looked in the local paper I asked Micky if the figure on the properties that were listed was the rent per year. 'No,' says Micky, 'that's how much it costs to buy!' I ended up buying a terraced house for £8,000 and Stoke-on-Trent became my adopted home. When Joanne and I moved into the house in February 1983, I soon learnt that £57 per week wasn't enough for us to live on, so I took a part-time job in Brian Rourke's cycle shop, which allowed me to train in the morning and work in the shop in the afternoon. Brian has built many of my bikes over the years and his bike shop is still going strong in Stoke and is well worth a visit if you are in the city.

I was one of three riders in the 1983 Moducel team, alongside Micky and Dudley Hayton. My first race for Moducel was a pro-am event in Ellesmere and it was the perfect start as I won, beating Mark Bell and Phil Thomas. The first pro win came in Wolverhampton a few weeks later when I took a stage of the Penn Two-Day race. I also rode the Kellogg's City Centre Cycling series, and those races are covered in the next chapter.

My second year as a pro, 1984, would give me one of the greatest moments in my career. In June, the British Professional Road Race was being held in the Isle of Man and as soon as the race venue was announced I began to look forward to it. There was pressure on me as I'd had some good results on home soil, having won the British Junior Road Race title and the Manx International. But the pro road race was something else again. The local papers were talking up my chances and being the local favourite meant that a lot of the guys in the race would be looking at me as one to watch. So there was pressure, but most of it was, as always, self-inflicted. I wanted to win even more than usual because the race would be in front of so many friends and my family. I didn't realise it at the time, but most of my best performances came in the Island or when I was racing through my adopted home town of Stoke. I had a fear of failure in races which I knew would be watched by friends or family and where I knew there would be more press attention on me.

The race was held at the end of Manx International Week and I'd already won two pro criteriums, so my confidence was high. The day before the road race I took Sid Barras, Bill Nickson, Keith Lambert, Ian Banbury and Nigel Dean, who were all there for the big race, out on a fishing trip in Douglas Bay. Bill was throwing up after about an hour on the boat and

Keith was next to follow suit. By the end of the trip there was only myself and Sid that felt okay. I remember Bill saying after the race that the fishing trip cost him the national title.

There had been some controversy before the race when five British riders who raced for continental teams – Paul Sherwen, Robert Millar, Sean Yates, Graham Jones and John Herety - decided not to turn up. The rumour was that the row was all to do with money, but whatever it was none of the five were on the start line on Douglas Promenade at half eight that Sunday morning. The race rolled out along the TT course and by the time we had reached the seven-mile mark at Ballacraine crossroads one rider, Dave Akam, had gone clear on his own. Dave was based in Italy and rode for the Gis team. He was soon joined by Steve Wakefield of the Modolo-Elswick team, but with the race being 117 miles no one was particularly worried by a breakaway so early on.

By the time they had reached Kirk Michael after eighteen miles of racing they had an advantage of more than three minutes, but Wakefield later punctured as the pair rode out of Ramsey and began the climb to Snaefell mountain. There had been a mix-up before the race which meant there were no neutral service cars. Neutral service vehicles are ones provided by the race organisers to give spare wheels or mechanical help to riders who haven't got their own team car, or who need help and their team car can't get to them. So Wakefield had to ride on with a flat tyre and lost ground on Akam, who pushed on over the mountain. As he came past the finish line for the first time in front of the TT Grandstand in Douglas he had a lead of more than six minutes. Then Akam began the first of twenty-one laps of a four-and-a-bit-mile circuit, starting and finishing in front of the Grandstand. By now Wakefield had been given a spare wheel from another team but there was no way he was going to catch Akam on his own and he hovered between the leader and the peloton.

As I sat in the peloton I had no idea of how well Akam was going, but with eighteen laps remaining – around seventy-five miles – Wakefield was swallowed up by the peloton. Yet we were not catching Akam; he was still riding strongly and maintaining his six-minute lead. There were a couple of attacks from the peloton, but the pace was still fast enough to prevent anyone else escaping. My Moducel teammate and fellow Manxman Nigel Dean went to the front to try and close the gap on Akam and got some help from Keith 'Legs' Lambert of the Falcon squad. With fourteen laps to go the injection of pace at the front of the bunch was taking effect, and Akam was beginning to pay the price for his brave effort. The lead was now below six minutes and Akam's cause was not helped when he had to swerve around some horses in the road.

As the gap closed, it encouraged riders in the bunch to believe that they could close and establish a lead group with Akam. Micky Morrison, my former Moducel team mate who was then with the ANC team, attacked and was joined by my teammate Ian Banbury. After around 85 miles in the lead, Akam was caught by the two chasers with just twenty-two miles remaining. The three leaders gained two minutes, which was not enough of an advantage for them with seven laps to go. With an hour or so of racing remaining, things were getting nervy and in the bunch there was a flurry of attacks, including one move which looked dangerous. It contained Raleigh's Malcolm Elliott, one of the pre-race favourites, and Bill Nickson, who was also capable of taking the title.

When the Elliott group had a lead of almost two minutes I thought the race was over. Luckily, I still had my Moducel teammate Nigel Dean with me and he dropped back down the group to find me. Nigel asked me how I was feeling and I told him I was still strong but I didn't want to commit myself too much into helping the chase of the break in case it all came back together for a bunch gallop. 'Just sit tight and hold on,' said Nigel, and then went straight to the front and led the chase for the last two laps.

We caught the break as they went around the final corner. They started messing around as none of them wanted to lead out the sprint, so were going about five miles an hour slower than the bunch. Instinct takes over in moments such as that; the sprinting blinkers came down and it was time for blast off. I went past Elliott as though he had a puncture and caught Nickson ten yards from the line. The next thing I knew I was freewheeling across the line with my arms in the air. Had I really just won the national title only a few hundred yards from where I grew up, and in front of all of my family? It seemed like a dream. Winning the pro title was amazing enough, but to do it in the Isle of Man seemed too good to be true. I've seen the TT Grandstand packed full of spectators for many sporting occasions but I've never seen a crowd like the one that greeted the finish of that race. It was just a sea of people.

The emotion that day was similar to when I won the Manx International in 1979, but the British pro road race was even more prestigious - and to win the national racing as a pro was a dream come true. It was only in the days and weeks that followed that I heard all of the stories about people leaving their Sunday dinners to go cold because they were listening to the race on Manx Radio and rushed to the Grandstand because there was a chance of seeing a Manx rider winning the title. Few of those spectators would have realised it at

Magical moments in front of my home crowd: Above - winning the 1984 British Professional Road Race. Below - with Nickson & Elliott on the podium

the time but my fear of failing in front of all those fans in the place in which I had grown up was a factor in my victory that day. I knew that if I was with the leaders in the sprint for the line no one was going to beat me.

When the British Road Race Championship came around in 1988. I wasn't in the best frame of mind. I'd got involved in a row over contracts with the Emmelle-MBK team and the Ever Ready squad. That had all begun at the end of the 1987 season when I was riding for Percy Bilton. It had a been a fantastic year for me, with a victory in the first Kellogg's Tour of Britain, which is covered in the next chapter. But Ron Groome, the boss of Percy Bilton, was not happy with some rumours that were circulating in the UK pro scene. There was talk of race fixing and of riders buying victories and of race organisers fixing races so that certain riders won. In particular, there was a rumour that some riders were involved in fixing the result of Sport For Television events, which were the races that got the TV coverage and were, therefore, the races that were most important to team sponsors. None of these allegations were aimed at the Percy Bilton team; all of us in the team knew how Ron felt about such things and there was no way any of us was going to throw a race for money.

Talking more generally about pro cycling, both in the UK and on the Continent, you would have to be pretty naïve to think that race fixing didn't happen or that certain riders didn't try to buy victories. It did go on, and there were occasions when I was offered money in the British road race by rivals who wanted me to sit up if I was away in a breakaway. I was one of the best sprinters around at the time and some riders felt that they had no chance against me in a sprint, so some thought the only way they could win was to offer me money. I never took the money; that British pro road champion's jersey was

Douglas Pro Crit, June 1984

worth much more to me than the money they were offering.
But from personal experience I knew that money was on offer
to try to buy a win so I wasn't surprised at the rumours about
riders trying to fix Sport For Television events.

Nothing was ever proved about the race fixing allegations,
but Ron felt that he had heard enough to convince him that
there was something going on. He had always told me and
the other guys in the team that if he thought any fixing was
going on he would withdraw sponsorship. We all knew
he was serious so never dared put a foot out of line. Ron
threatened to withdraw sponsorship from the Percy Bilton
team. In the end Percy Bilton did run a team in 1988, but in
the winter of 1987-88 it looked to me that there would be
no Percy Bilton team racing in the upcoming season and I
needed to find a new team.

In December 1987 I was still without a definite contract

for the following year. I was a pro bike rider with a family to support and a mortgage and bills to pay. I needed another contract. So when I got a call from Sid Barras, who was managing the Emmelle team, I was interested. We discussed things over the phone and he offered me a contract of £10,000 for the 1988 season. It was around a £5,000 a year pay cut on my 1987 contract, but I thought it was better than nothing so made a verbal agreement with Sid over the phone. Of course, Sod's Law then came into play and a day or so after I'd made that verbal agreement with Sid I received a phone call from Mick Bennett, who was the manager of the Ever Ready team. He was offering much more than Emmelle were, and Ever Ready would pay me expenses and give me a car. Added to that was the fact that Ever Ready had a strong team that I knew would support me. Tony Doyle, Glenn Clarke, Phil Bayton and Jon Walshaw were in the squad and I felt that Ever Ready was a better unit than Emmelle, so it was not just about the money. As I hadn't actually signed a contract with Emmelle, I felt that I could still reject the verbal agreement and sign with Ever Ready. A pro bike rider's career is tough and you only have a few years to make the most that you can. I felt it was the right decision.

So I went to meet Mick at a service station on the M6 and signed a contract to ride for Ever Ready. Following my decision, Emmelle threatened to disband its team because I had decided not to ride. This put me in a very awkward position; it was as though I was being blamed for the Emmelle riders losing their jobs. The Professional Cycling Association (PCA) fined me £1,000 for bringing the sport into disrepute. I didn't agree with the decision and put in an appeal. I was represented by a solicitor called Mike Townley, who did a great job and tore the PCA's case to shreds. I won the appeal over the fine which was reduced to £125. I made sure I got back the £75 it had cost me to put in the appeal.

Looking back, I think that although I had made a verbal agreement I was not committed to anything until I signed a contract. I think the decision I made to sign for Ever Ready was the same decision most people would make if they had a family to support and the knowledge that bike racing was a short and dangerous career. I feel the PCA made a point of taking action against me simply because I was the highest profile rider in the UK at that time. If I hadn't won as many races, they wouldn't have bothered making an issue out of the contract dispute. The dispute got quite a lot of coverage in the cycling media and it was something I didn't need as I tried to prepare for the 1988 season. When I finally knew which team I would be racing for that year, things didn't go well and as the national road race approached I had little to celebrate.

The race was in Newport, Shropshire, and finished in the town centre on part of the circuit which in recent years has been used for the popular Newport Nocturne event organised by Mick Jeggo. The Nocturne even has a 'Past Masters' event which I raced in a couple of years ago. If there was one advantage to be had of not having brilliant form and having my preparation disrupted by contract disputes, it was that no one really expected me to do anything in Newport. As the race drew nearer, I was not confident and was even considering talking to the team boss about changing my role. Maybe it was time for me to become a team player, or a domestique, as we say in cycling. I was beginning to think that I couldn't ask others to help me win races any longer and that it was time to give up the role I had as a team leader. This was my mindset going into the race, but it was decided before the race that I was still the best bet for a win in the Ever Ready-Ammoco team.

Two weeks before the race, I went to Portugal for a training camp with Tony Doyle, who was preparing for the World Track Championships in which he would ride the individual pursuit. Tony had twice been world pursuit champion and would win a silver medal in 1988. Glenn Clarke joined us as well and we did eight days of training. With Tony's speed in the pursuit, training with him was perfect preparation for riding criteriums, which involved constant accelerations out of corners and are always raced all out from the gun. Tony had a very technical approach to training and I learned a lot from him. He used to do power sessions which I found really brought on good form. We would find a circuit of about 5kms but with a 3km climb and a 2km descent. We would go up this climb in a big gear, maybe 52x14, while sitting in the saddle and so not making it easier by standing on the pedals and using your body weight to help. It was like doing weight training on the bike, pushing this big gear and tying the handlebars in knots as we gripped onto the bike to get as much leverage as possible. We'd spin a small gear on the descent then go up the climb again but knock it up one gear so we would ride it in the 52x13. We would do this power session in the evening after riding three and a half hours in the morning at an average of about 25mph.

I came back from that training camp with unbelievable form. After heaving those big gears up the climb in Portugal I couldn't feel my legs at all when I was on the bike, it felt that easy. After the contract wrangles of the previous winter, it felt fantastic. However, my mood dampened when I heard that someone had reported me and a few other pros to the taxman, accusing us of dodging tax by being paid cash and not declaring it. With being born and raised in the Isle of Man, known to most of the world as a 'tax haven', the Inland Revenue had a particular interest in me. The tax inspector went through my books with a fine tooth comb. Having to sort all that out distracted me a little from my racing, although I rode well at the British Criterium Championship in Leek, Staffordshire. Despite being something of a specialist in crits, I'd never won the national title, in fact I'd never won a medal of any kind. It was a race I really wanted to win because the structure of UK racing at that time meant there were far more crits than road races, so the crit champion got to show off the British jersey far more often than the road race champion. I came home with a silver medal, but the good thing about the ride was that it proved I was in good form.

When the national road race came round I remember feeling a strange numbness in my legs. Even on the climbs I couldn't feel any effort or fatigue. It was one of those times when cycling seemed easy. A rare thing. Our Ever Ready squad was smaller in number than most of the other teams in the race. Raleigh-Banana, PMS-Dawes, Percy Bilton and Emmelle-MBK all had more riders than us. But the three other guys in my team were prepared to ride their socks off and that's what they did that day. Even though he was nearing the end of his career Phil Bayton, the Staffordshire Engine, still had as much horse power as the Flying Scotsman. We also had Jon Walshaw, who was a first year pro but put in a good ride. The final member of our team was a class act. Tony Doyle, the former world pro pursuit champion and star of the six-day track events, enabled me to have a relatively easy ride in the first half of the race. Despite suffering from a hip injury after a crash in Ireland the week before, Tony was able to stay with me and keep me in his wheel until he packed in at half distance.

When a group went clear and gained almost three minutes, I felt strong enough to cross the gap alone. Even though I had built my reputation as a sprinter, I knew that on my day I could ride a good time-trial and I put that quality to good use. I caught them at the bottom of Cheney Hill and put in a big effort all the way up the climb. By the time I reached the top only Chris Lilywhite (Raleigh-Banana), Nick Barnes (PMS-Falcon) and my old mate Mike Doyle (PMS-Dawes) were still with me. I was made up when I saw Mike there, but sadly he got dropped before we reached the finish. In the last kilometre the bunch was only 500 yards behind and there was a bit of messing about at the finish, as Lilywhite and Barnes tried to outwit me in the sprint. But even if they'd had motorbikes they weren't going to beat me. I won the sprint easily, with Barnes second and Lilywhite third. It was an emotional win, not just because of the prestige of being British champion again, but because I'd had a crap year with problems off the bike and little to celebrate on it.

To be a pro bike rider takes so much time and effort. You have to devote your life to it. To give all that and come up with poor results is hard to take, and having to deal with the contract wrangles in the winter had me wondering if all the effort in training and racing was worthwhile. In the months leading up to that national road race win, I'd been losing my enthusiasm for racing. It seemed as though there were more bad times than good. But the good times do make up for all those hard times and, having had a bad year, it made victory that much sweeter. I was a winner and always needed to get results. To have a bit of a lean year and then suddenly 'bang', and I'm British champion again, was a special moment.

Before the Kellogg's Tour of Britain came along in 1987

Winning the 1988 British Professional Road Race title in Newport, Shropshire

there were two main targets for UK-based pro riders - the British national title and the Milk Race. I won my first Milk Race stage as an amateur in 1981 but it was an event that was always special to race in, as it had an international reputation and attracted some of the world's best riders.

I won in Blackpool and Westminster in the 1986 Milk Race, which featured the fearsome Djamolidine 'Tashkent Tornado' Abdoujaparov. Details of that stage win are in the 'Friends and Rivals' chapter. I was never going to win the race overall, as I'd always have at least one day where I'd lose twenty minutes on a hilly stage. Two weeks was too long for me; I could win five-day stage races, but that was my limit as far as being a contender on general classification was concerned.

But I was a consistent finisher in the Milk Race, and only ever abandoned it once and that was in 1987 when I was part of the Percy Bilton team. One of my teammates, Mark Walsham, tested positive for codeine which he had inadvertently taken in a cold remedy and was thrown out of the race. That incident flattened me mentally and we had discussions about pulling the entire team out of the race. The whole affair left me feeling down and I was angry that Walsham's actions had ended up affecting the team. My heart wasn't in the race after that, and I climbed off a few days later.

When the Milk Race ended in 1993, British cycling lost an institution. It had a history and image that had been built up over decades and was a race that reached beyond die-hard cycling fans to the casual sports fans, who would come and watch if it happened to be in their town. It was a sad day when it ended and its demise may have been accelerated by the emergence of the Kellogg's Pro Tour of Britain, which was a race that was to give me the greatest victory in my professional career.

Crossing the line to win the Liverpool stage of the 1989 Milk Race ahead of the American 7-Eleven rider Roy Knickman

Some of the things photographers ask you to do! Before a Milk Race stage in my adopted home town of Stoke in 1989

STAGE 7
Cereal Killers

Cycling in the UK has never enjoyed the high profile it has in Europe. For a lot of historical reasons, cycling has always been a niche sport compared with football, cricket or rugby. But in the 1980s things began to change when Channel 4 gave major coverage to cycling, with daily highlights of the Tour de France and coverage of the Kellogg's City Centre Cycling series. Before Channel 4 came along, most cycling fans had to settle for a few minutes of weekly highlights of the Tour de France on ITV's World of Sport and coverage of cycling at the Olympics.

Channel 4 did a lot to raise the profile of the sport in the UK and I for one am glad that they did, and the Kellogg's City Centre Cycling series was a great way to promote the sport. In a country that has no cycling culture, the Kellogg's races were ideal. Even now, the Tour de France is a mystery to many UK sports fans. How often have you heard people wonder how Mark Cavendish can win six stages in one race and not win the Tour de France? Or how someone can win the Tour de France without ever winning one individual stage? Stage racing is complex; it's not just one race but several races within a race, and this is hard to explain to someone coming across the sport for the first time.

In countries which don't have the kind of cycling culture that exists in France, Belgium and Italy it's difficult for the average person in the street to understand the tactics. I've even spoken to a doctor I know, obviously a very intelligent guy, who has difficulty with the fact that a rider can be leading a stage of the Tour de France by as much as 20 minutes and still get caught. For him, and others like him, it seems bizarre and incomparable to other sports which are point-to-point races.

If an elite marathon runner had a twenty-minute head start he would always win – but the mechanics of cycling mean that there is more advantage to be had by riding in a group than there is with marathoners running in a group, so it's possible for cyclists to get a big lead and still be caught. It is possible to explain all these tactical complexities but it takes time and means that it's not easy for cycling to acquire new fans if you do it by focusing on stage races. When people ask me to explain the tactics of cycling and why a group can ride so much faster than one rider on their own, I make a suggestion. I tell them that next time they are a passenger in a car they should stick their head out of the window at 40mph and feel the force of the wind in their face. That's the kind of force a rider has to push against for mile after mile if they are in a solo break.

While stage racing is complex and difficult to understand, city centre circuit races, or criteriums, are different in that there are few breakaways and the guy that crosses the line first is the winner and the series will be won by the guy who wins the most individual races. In the UK, where football will always be the national sport, the Kellogg's series fitted in well with the culture, with races lasting around the same time as a football match, rather than going on for five or six hours as stages of a tour do.

Races were on small circuits right in the centre of towns and cities. They took place in the early evening, when town centres would usually be busy anyway. So the races went to the people rather than getting fans to stand on a hillside for hours waiting for a race to flash past. The Kellogg's races allowed fans to go to a bar and have a drink and then stand outside and watch the race go past every few minutes. That's why the Kellogg's series was so good for promoting the sport and a factor in why it proved so popular and attracted crowds the size of those you would usually see at football matches. Spectators only had to understand that the races lasted a certain number of laps and the first guy over the line at the finish was the winner. But while the races were simple, they were no less impressive in terms of how they tested a rider's fitness, riding skills and courage.

For me, the Kellogg's races were perfect and provided some of the greatest moments I had on a bike. I won four Kellogg's crits and was second overall once and third overall twice in the series which was made up of races across the UK during the summer. Yet at first I was fairly laid back about the prospect of the Kellogg's series. Even though it had TV coverage, no one was sure whether the series would be popular. To be honest, most of the UK pros were sceptical when it began as a televised event in 1983. I suppose we had all been in cycling long enough to know that all the promises made by sponsors or race organisers had to be taken with a pinch of salt. But as the races approached it seemed as if this new series was going to be different.

Today, with so many digital channels, it's possible to see a lot of cycling on TV but back in the 1980s the UK only had four television channels, so for one of those four to devote an hour every Monday evening to a UK cycle race was a dream come true for team sponsors who were desperate to get TV coverage. Another aspect which made the Kellogg's series stand out was the participation of some top international riders. Sean Kelly, Stephen Roche, Phil Anderson, Robert Millar, Allan Peiper and Freddie Maertens were some of the big names involved. Racing against the top continental guys in crits on British soil was unusual for us UK-based pros. As there was little TV coverage of cycling in the UK, the Kellogg's series suddenly became a major target for us as we knew the sponsors wanted to get the maximum amount of publicity. When I first heard that these big names were coming over I thought they would just turn up and take the appearance money without putting in too much effort to win. For most of them, the Kellogg's crits held little prestige compared with riding the Grand Tours or famous one-day classics.

But when guys such as Kelly, Roche, Anderson and Peiper arrived they showed that they were there to compete and always put on a fantastic show. There was no question of them just riding around and collecting their appearance money. And when the Kellogg's series began to catch on and attract big crowds, it just made the events even more exciting to race in and the level of competition increased too.

The first event in the Kellogg's series was at Bristol in 1983 and featured Sean Kelly, who at the time was the number one ranked rider in the world. He was joined by two more big names from the continental peloton – the Irishman Stephen Roche and the great Italian Francesco Moser.

When I arrived at the circuit in Bristol city centre any scepticism I may have had about this new series disappeared when I saw the professional set up and the huge crowds that had turned out to enjoy a bike race on a summer evening. In 2009, ITV's The Tour series used a similar format to the Kellogg's series, with ten city centre races in the summertime.

It's always good to see new events to promote cycling in the UK but with all due respect to the organisers and the riders I have to say that the crowds that turned out were nothing compared to what I saw in the Kellogg's series twenty odd years ago.

So in Bristol on that first night all the UK riders knew that this was going to be something else. For me, it would mean testing myself against some of the best riders in the world and I have to admit that I felt a bit intimidated when I looked around on the start line and saw Kelly, Roche and Moser. I remembered watching Moser win the World Road Race Championships and Paris-Roubaix and all of a sudden there I was about to race against a real legend of the sport.

That night in Bristol was the most intense race that I have ever been in. Right from the start it was full on; there was no let up in the pace, with attacks going all the time. The speed was unbelievable and, with the circuit being so tight, the required level of concentration demanded as much energy as turning the pedals with your legs. It is the only race I have ever finished where my eyes ached as much as my legs.

Effectively, the Kellogg's crits were like a one-hour lead out for a bunch sprint. There was no margin for error, a moment's lack of concentration could mean you crashing or losing the wheel in front and never getting it back. That first Kellogg's crit was raced at an average speed of 31mph on a circuit which had three tight bends, which meant three slow corners on each lap.

Phil Thomas, a UK-based pro, won in Bristol ahead of Phil Anderson, who was riding on the Continent for the Peugeot pro team. I was sixth, but wasn't too disappointed because the night had proved that I and other UK pros could compete against the best in the world in criteriums. Also, it was a fantastic race due to the atmosphere created by the big crowd and the quality of the riders in the field. The Bristol race just made me even more motivated when the next Kellogg's race came around. To make sure I was in the best form possible for criteriums, I would train behind a motorbike on the road. That was frowned upon a bit in the UK, so when I could I would go back to the Isle of Man to do this type of training. I would go from Douglas to Peel, a run of eleven miles from one side of the Island to the other. I'd do this ride, from Douglas to Peel and back, in about thirty-eight minutes on a good day. This type of high speed training was ideal for the physical demands of the Kellogg's criteriums.

I had to wait until 1984 for my first Kellogg's series win, which came in Manchester. That was an amazing night, with crowds five and ten deep in places. The noise was deafening and even Hugh Porter, who was doing the commentary over the PA system, was drowned out by the sound of all the fans around the circuit shouting and screaming. Even now it makes the hairs on the back of my neck stand up when I think about it. The adrenalin rush was a mixture of excitement and fear. Sean Kelly was in the race, so I got a sense of achievement beating a man who was one of the best road racers and best sprinters in the world. In Glasgow, I beat the local hero Robert Millar, who had finished fourth in the 1984 Tour de France and won the King of the Mountains competition. I was always consistent in the Kellogg's races, so it was a bit of a disappointment not to win the series overall.

As the Kellogg's series progressed, there was rivalry between us UK-based pros and the continental guys. Some of this rivalry was influenced by the fact that the UK riders got a flat rate while the continental stars were paid much more in appearance money in order to persuade them to come over and race. So we had a race in which the UK riders, who made up the majority of the field, felt that they were the ones putting the show on and getting much less reward than the handful of continental stars. The rivalry was hyped up a lot at the time, but it wasn't that big a deal to us.

The Kellogg's series also showed how the profile of continental racing was changing, as it was in the early 1980s that there was the first real challenge to the European domination of the sport. As well as UK and American riders making their mark on road racing, there was an invasion of Australian riders, many of whom raced in the Kellogg's series. Phil Anderson was the best of the bunch and in 1981 became the first Aussie to wear the yellow jersey in the Tour de France. Phil was an animal, very tough to race against and a guy who always wanted to win. He won Kellogg's crits, but never managed to win the whole series. But he certainly made his mark and in 1983 lapped the whole field on the tough circuit in Birmingham.

Allan Peiper, too, was a very aggressive rider who had success in the UK and became a popular rider with fans. Some overseas riders couldn't handle the speed and intensity of the Kellogg's crits but Anderson and Peiper were two that could. They could have come over and taken the money and not really tried to compete but both of them gave it 100 per cent in all of the races which helped make them a great spectacle. Another Aussie arrival was Shane Sutton, who is now a key figure in the success of British riders on road and track. Shane arrived in England hellbent on becoming a pro rider and he pitched up in the West Midlands where he would often be seen out training up and down the congested roads of industrial England. With his sun-bleached long hair and moustache and his cocky, no-nonsense attitude, Shane was the Crocodile Dundee of cycling – all he needed was an old-style cycling crash hat with corks hanging off it.

The Aussies were all tough characters; if you had travelled half way across the world to make it in a sport where few of their countrymen had ever made a mark, you would have to be tough. I used to train with Shane and he was great to ride with but you always had a thought in the back of your mind that anything could happen when he was around.

I remember one morning when Steve Jones and I were training with Shane and a bus cut us up, not an unusual occurrence, and one that would usually prompt an appropriate hand gesture to the driver or a few choice words shouted out. But this wasn't enough for Shane; the bus driver was in the wrong and he was going to make sure he knew it. Shane rode after the bus and when it pulled up at a stop he jumped off his bike and leapt on board to have it out with the driver. Shane was in the driver's face giving him a piece of his mind and advising him to be more courteous to other road users in his own inimitable way. The bus driver then pulled away, with Shane still on board giving him what for while I was with Steve holding Shane's bike. Steve then had to chase after the bus for two miles towing Shane's bike alongside him.

I got on well with Shane even though we were big rivals. We respected each other's ability as bike riders and you could be sure there would never be a dull moment with him around. He was always full of energy and enthusiasm, and those qualities are still evident when you hear him talking about his current involvement with the British cycling team. He lives and breathes cycling and it's no surprise that many of the young riders he now guides in the British set-up so often speak of how infectious his enthusiasm can be.

Looking back on the Kellogg's series twenty years on, they

are still fresh in the memory and were fantastic events for riders and spectators alike. In recent years it has become more and more difficult to organise point-to-point road races in the UK due to ever-increasing problems with traffic congestion and getting local authorities and police to sanction the necessary road closures. To me, this merely emphasises the appeal of city centre criteriums, as they are easier to organise and are easier for the casual sports fan to understand. Having said that, I think it will be difficult to recapture the glory days of the Kellogg's races. There was something special about that era in British cycling and about those races in particular. It was sad that the series didn't continue. I think there was a fantastic opportunity to make it an international event, taking races to major cities around the world and run it in a similar way to Formula 1 Grand Prix racing. While it was great to see a big sponsor backing racing in the UK, I think it was a mistake to abandon the series in 1987 and replace it with the Kellogg's-sponsored professional Tour of Britain. Yet the Tour was popular too, for a time, and I had my own moment of glory in the first tour in 1987.

The first Kellogg's Pro Tour was a massive event for British cycling. Even though I think it would have been better for the sport in the UK to have continued and developed the criterium series, there is no denying that the Kellogg's Tour got off to a great start. The City Centre series had won a whole new audience for cycling and these new spectators now had a chance to watch many of the riders who had become familiar in criterium races on TV battling it out in a stage race. Sean Kelly was the biggest name in the race but there was a long list of riders who raced in the Tour de France and other major continental events. Steven Rooks, the Dutchman who would win the King of the Mountains prize in the Tour de France in 1988, was there alongside the Aussie Allan Peiper and Frenchman Denis Roux. Ludo Peeters, Paul Haghedooren, Phillippe Casado and Michele Vermotte were names that Channel 4 viewers had become used to hearing Phil Liggett call out in the station's Tour de France coverage. Now they were all riding on British roads in a big stage race and only three weeks after TV viewers had watched the Tour de France finish in Paris. It was exciting to be in that first pro tour and it certainly caught the imagination of the British public. When Sid Barras, then thirty-nine, rode over Fleet Moss on his own in the Yorkshire leg it looked for all the world like a stage of the Tour de France as the huge crowds parted like the Red Sea as he made his way up the climb.

In 1987 I was riding for Percy Bilton and for our squad, not to mention the other UK-based pro teams, the Kellogg's Tour was the big event of the year. The field was probably the best ever assembled for a UK race, apart from when Britain hosted the World Road Race Championships at Goodwood in 1982. Despite the quality of the field, I was confident that I could still win a stage.

I had my eye on the third stage from Manchester to Birmingham, which passed through my adopted home town of Stoke-on-Trent. The day before was a brutal stage from Newcastle to Manchester, a hilly stage of 170 miles which seemed to include every peak between Tyneside and Lancashire. That stage was the longest ever in a UK stage race. Maybe the organisers put it in to show that the country could hold stages that were as long as those in the Tour de France. Whatever the reason, it was a tortuous day. Barras got huge cheers as he climbed Fleet Moss in pursuit of the Dutchman Steven Rooks, who had been away on his own for most of the day. Barras and Rooks were caught by a chase group before the descent into Manchester and it was Joey McLoughlin who crossed the line first after eight hours of racing. I came in twenty minutes later and was in bits. It was getting dark by the time me and the rest of the main field crossed the line and I remember that I didn't get a post-race massage until half eleven that night. Hardly the ideal preparation for my attempt to win stage three, but as often happened in my career I would have one awful day followed by a brilliant one.

Stage three from Manchester to Birmingham on August 20 was a 111-mile stage. The race took in four laps of Stoke city centre at around half-distance so spectators there could get a good look at the race. The circuit included a steep climb called Penkhull Hill and my first thought was that I didn't want to suffer the embarrassment of being dropped on a circuit in my home town. A rider can find many things to motivate them in a race, and that day one of my driving forces was fear.

So, when the stage began under grey skies in Manchester, I was a worried man because of the previous day's battering. Yet the stage started well and after fourteen miles I took second place in a King of the Mountains prime in Buxton behind Frenchman Denis Roux of the Peugeot team. By the time we got to Leek, I had made it into a nine-man breakaway which looked strong enough to stay clear all the way to Birmingham. In the group were the British riders Malcolm Elliott and Adrian Timmis, who had both just returned from finishing the Tour de France. They were with Tony Capper's ANC-Halfords team, which was the only British team to compete on the Continent. They were two strong riders, but Malcolm was the one I feared most as I knew he would have a decent sprint at the end of the stage. Also in the break were Frenchmen Frederic Garnier (Toshiba) and Michel Bibollet

(RMO); Belgian Paul Haghedooren (Sigma); Switzerland's Joerg Muller (PDM); Dutchman Marc van Orsouw (PDM) and Aussie Stephen Hodge (Kas). Finally there was British pro Stuart Coles of the Interent-Yugo team who, up to that point in the Kellogg's Tour, had felt that he was out of his depth and had phoned his dad after the Manchester stage to say that he wanted to go home to Wales.

The break was short-lived and when we were caught my Percy Bilton teammate Neil Martin attacked as we approached Stoke-on-Trent because his wife Maria was waiting in the city to cheer him on. He was going away from us, but I was soon chasing in a group with Coles, British rider Paul Watson (Lycra-Halfords) and Kvetoslav Palov (ANC-Halfords). We began to close the gap on Neil, who had a bit of bad luck when he was held up by a railway level crossing. The gate was closed so he had to stop and the race officials noted the time gap when he stopped and set us all off with the same gaps when the gates were raised.

As we neared Birmingham there were six of us in the lead group with me, my teammate Neil Martin, Timmis and Coles. Our advantage over the peloton was now enough to put Timmis in the race lead. The overnight leader Steven Rooks sensed the danger and his strong PDM team began to drive the chase. The lead was tumbling, from a peak of three minutes it was now less than ninety seconds. Coles was the first to make a move from the group and it was a surprise as he had struggled in the race and had only turned pro that season. But he was obviously feeling strong and I saw him go and immediately got on to his wheel. Now there was just two of us left and we worked together to maintain our lead, knowing that there were four laps of a tight circuit around Birmingham to come. Once we got onto the finishing circuit with a good lead over the chasers, I knew the race was mine. There was a bit of cat and mouse in the final straight but as soon as I launched my sprint it was all over.

'The Pocket Rocket is warming up for take-off,' said Phil Liggett on the Tour of Britain highlights show that evening. 'He comes through ever so easily, grits his teeth and tears that bike apart.'

I crossed the line with my arms pointing straight to the heavens for what was the greatest win of my career. Even though I won two British road race titles, the calibre of the field in the Kellogg's Tour made it my best win as a pro.

STAGE 8
Friends and rivals

There's camaraderie in pro cycling, as you spend a lot of time training and racing with the same riders. When you are not doing that you are travelling or living out of a suitcase in hotels. You get to know teammates and rivals whether you want to or not. Some you get on with, and some you don't. I was lucky to have raced with and against some great riders and great characters.

There was Phil Thomas, the man all of the riders of my generation knew as The Maggot. Phil was a typical Scouser, always looking for an advantage, someone who we used to joke would kill his own grandmother if it meant he could win a race. To an extent I had some of the same qualities in terms of being ruthless in wanting to win. Phil used to let his mouth run away with him a bit too much at times, but at heart he was harmless. He just wanted to win races like we all did and as we often used to end up contesting sprint finishes he was a guy I had many battles against.

Stories about Phil are legendary, although many of them may have been a little embellished over the years. But it's true to say he was a tough man to beat. Physically, he may not have been the greatest rider in the world and his career was constantly hampered by the fact that he was an asthma sufferer. Tactically, he was brilliant, and this won him a lot of races even if sometimes his tactics pushed the rule book to its limit. Yet take a look at the record books and you will see some impressive victories. In the hard-fought Kellogg's City Centre series he won the first two series in 1983 and 1984, beating such riders as Sean Kelly and Phil Anderson. No mean feat. It wasn't unknown for Phil to lean on riders or flick someone (swerve slightly) in a sprint in order to stop anyone getting past him. He could be a little dirty in the bunch gallops and would tend to push you into the barriers, which was a tactic that angered many of the riders who took him on. But for Phil that was all part of the game. I ended up coming to blows with him in one race of a Michelin-sponsored criterium. We were winding up for the sprint and he grabbed my shorts to pull me back so I gave him a back hander and caught him right in the ribs, which knocked the wind out of his sails and he went backwards. Like all riders who do well in criteriums, he was a good bike handler but he also had a fantastic racing brain too. In the first few years of my pro career it was hard for me to beat him, but after about 1986 he started to get a bit slower and I tended to have the edge over him.

The city of Liverpool has produced some great riders over the years and in the 1980s Phil Thomas and Joey McCloughlin emerged and achieved good results. If you could have combined the tactical nous of Thomas with the physical ability of McCloughlin, I reckon we would have seen the first Scouser to win the World Road Race Championship.

Malcolm Elliott from Sheffield was another of my main rivals in the 1980s and he was probably the most naturally talented bike rider Britain has ever produced. I always found him to be quite a shy character, but he got a reputation for being a bit of playboy, an image which Malcolm has gone on record as saying was a label given to him by the media, and not one that he thought was fair. There is no doubt, however, that he always looked the part; you'd never catch him wearing dirty socks, that's for sure. He was always immaculately turned out back then just as he is now. It's amazing to think that he is still racing as a professional in the UK at the age of forty-eight and that fact just highlights his tremendous ability. Malcolm won a lot of big races, including stages of the Tour of Spain and the points jersey. Add to that wins in the Milk Race, Kellogg's Pro Tour of Britain and the Nissan Classic Tour of Ireland and it is obvious he was a class act. He would have won the Amstel Gold Race too, had he not found himself in a group where all the other riders were Dutch and so got worked over by riders from rival teams who would rather see a home win than let a British rider win the Amstel for the first time.

Even with his impressive palmares, I always felt that Malcolm never achieved as much as he could. Winning seemed to come easy for him. He was always so relaxed and laid back before races. I remember sharing a room with him during the Sealink International and thirty minutes before the race was due to start he would be lying on his bed in the hotel listening to his Walkman while most of the other riders would be rushing around making sure they were ready for the day's racing. Malcolm just oozed ability, and he was a world-class cyclist. To be honest, I think he was too laid back, and that meant that he never realised his true potential. He relied so much on his natural ability and could win races without having to train as hard as he could; if he had put that work in, I think he could have won the green jersey in the Tour de France and maybe even have become the second British man to win the World Road Race Championship. He really was that good. Malcolm probably trains harder now in his second pro career than he did in the 1980s during his first. Back then, it was possible to make a good living as a UK-based pro rider and this may also have been a factor in his career path. There was a lucrative pro circuit in the USA too, and that's where Malcolm saw out the final years of his career, before he came out of retirement at the age of forty-two. He's still racing and winning now, which is a testimony to his incredible talent.

One of the strongest guys I ever came across on the bike was Phil Bayton, the 'Staffordshire Engine'. I raced with him in the Moducel team and with Ever Ready and he was as strong as an ox. He was also the tidiest bike rider I've ever known. Some pro riders are so disorganised that I used to wonder how they ever got to races on time. But Phil was Mr Organised. When he opened his suitcase at a hotel everything would be immaculately packed. It was like he'd been trained to pack the case by James Bond. His jerseys, shoes and shorts would all have to go in the exact place. Being that organised saves time for a rider and saving time means saving energy, because you'll never be running around at the last minute trying to find something you need for that day's racing when you could be lying on the bed getting a few more minutes' rest. Phil made being organised into an art form. His favourite trick was to bet his roommate that he could find something in his suitcase while blindfolded. Whatever you named in his case, he'd be able to pick it up straight away because he'd memorised where everything went. His bikes were always immaculate too. I was a stickler for my bikes being clean and set up perfectly, but Phil took it to a whole new level.

I went to his house once and his garage was like an art gallery for bikes. All of these gleaming machines set out in a line with all of his shoes neatly arranged too. Whenever we turned up for a race Phil would always inspect your bike. He'd even squeeze the brake lever and have a look to see if you had cleaned inside the lever hood. Phil is a great bloke and a great rider. Anyone who remembers the 1973 Milan-San Remo will know that. It's the longest classic in the calendar now, and although back then there were longer races, it was still 180 miles. Phil was riding for TI Raleigh that year and he and his teammate Dave Lloyd attacked after just one kilometre. It was madness, but the pair of them built up a lead of eight minutes and spent four and a half hours alone in the lead. It was great for the sponsors, getting two of their riders on TV for all that time, but it was always doomed to failure and they got caught after spending more than 100 miles holding off the cream of European cycling. That ride was typical Phil. All he ever wanted to do was mash a huge gear all day; he wasn't happy unless he was hammering along at 35mph.

That eagerness to go on the attack could be frustrating for his managers and teammates. If Phil could have saved his power for the final miles of races more often, as opposed to attacking early, he would have won more races. But in the 1980s UK cycling fans came to enjoy seeing Phil dragging pelotons up and down the country for mile upon mile and I'm sure he got a sense of satisfaction when he saw that he was strong enough to string a peloton of 100 or more riders out into one long line with everyone on the rivet trying to hang on.

I remember when Phil and I were riding with Moducel at a circuit race in Ireland. Phil was in top form and before the race Sid Barras, our team captain, asked him to save himself for the finish because he knew that if Bayton attacked and got a gap at the end of race, no one was going to catch him. 'I don't want to see you until ten laps to go,' said Sid. He wanted Phil to hide in the bunch and conserve his energy for the final laps. Sid told Phil that even if he got away in a group towards the end it was okay, as long as there were no sprinters in the group that could beat Phil in the gallop. Phil said 'okay', but as soon as the flag went down he was off up the road taking a few sprinters with him in a group and, to be fair, Phil wasn't a sprinter so had little chance of winning. It was frustrating at the time, but funny now I look back on it.

Phil was the original 'bunch engine' and all he ever wanted to do was ride flat out all the time. As soon as the flag went he was on the big ring riding on the rivet at 35mph. He was a great guy for a sponsor who wanted to back an individual rider because you could guarantee he would get on TV at some point during the race. I still see Phil at races occasionally. In 2008 I was driving a press car at the Tour of Britain and I was taking photographers to different locations to get photos of the stages. One day I was driving along and saw a cyclist 500 metres ahead going the same way as us and obviously going out to watch the race. It had been two decades since I raced with Phil but as soon as I saw him I recognised him. His head was slightly to one side and his elbow flicking out. I drew alongside him and sure enough he was in the big ring and riding flat out on the rivet just as he did when he was racing. He was shooting from one location to another to see the stage more than once. There was a headwind that day but he was still doing 35mph. There are still a few more miles left in the Staffordshire Engine's tank.

If Phil was the tidiest and most organised bike rider I've ever come across, then my old mates 'Super' Sid Barras and Keith 'Legs' Lambert were probably the most disorganised. Sid and Keith lived near to each other and would often travel to races together. They once turned up at a pro race in a van packed with all their stuff, which they set about unpacking. Suitcases? 'Got them,' they said. Kit bags? 'Check.' But there were two things missing. They'd both forgotten to put their race bikes in the van! If they were any more laid back they would have been horizontal. Sid is one of the best riders Britain has ever produced and a great guy to ride with and against. He was a great sprinter and we had some fantastic battles over the years. But Sid was lucky that he had his wife Linda behind him because he'd have forgotten to turn up for races half the time if it wasn't for her.

Mark Bell was another character and one of many riders of that era who emerged from Merseyside. He was probably the most talented of the bunch and on his day could be a brilliant rider, as he was when he won the British amateur road race title in 1981 and the British professional title in 1986 when riding for Raleigh-Banana. I had some great laughs with Mark, who had the same kind of mischievous character as I did. One night we were sharing a room at a hotel in York during a race and it was a really hot and humid night so all the guests had their windows open. Our room was on a corner, which gave us a good spot to fire missiles at other rooms. The soigneur had left a big box of oranges in our room and we spent the night throwing the oranges at the windows and watching them make the curtains billow. We'd hide like a couple of school kids as the people in the other rooms came to the window to find out where the oranges had come from. That was another relic of the Dennis the Menace-type kid I was; part of me never grew up. Maybe that's true of most pro bike riders, who spend their lives doing something most people give up doing when they are kids.

One of our favourite tricks was raiding hotel mini-bars. We'd have a can of Coke and empty a bottle of vodka or gin into it from the mini-bar and then top the bottle up with water and put it back in the mini-bar. We'd perfected the art of pushing the seal back up so it looked like no-one had opened it so we didn't get billed for it. The team manager would come in to the room and see us sipping Coke but we'd be trying to hide a cheeky grin because we knew we were getting away with something we shouldn't be doing, especially during a stage race such as the Milk Race. Of course, this trick is no use now as most hotels have an electronic system which automatically registers a sale when someone takes a drink from the mini-bar. Spoilsports.

At the time antics like that were just fun, but both Mark and I were to suffer the effects of drink problems later in life. Sadly, Mark succumbed to the effects of his drinking and died at the tragically young age of 48 in 2009.

Perhaps the most famous, or maybe infamous, rival that I faced was Djamolidine Abdoujaparov, or the 'Tashkent Tornado' as he was known. In the 1990s he became the most feared sprinter in the world and won the green points jersey in the Tour de France three times. But he was as ruthless and dangerous as he was fast. Before he made it big in continental racing he raced as an amateur and turned up at the pro-am Milk Race. I was riding for the Percy Bilton team in 1986 and the opening stage was a 140-mile epic from Birmingham to Blackpool. We came into the finish along the Golden Mile on Blackpool seafront and along the right-hand side of the road. It was a massive bunch sprint and as we got within sight of the line a gap opened up in front of me between a rider and a line of parked cars. There wasn't much room, but all sprinters will tell you that they see gaps where others just see riders or other obstacles. It's an instinct; you have to react immediately and without thinking of any negative consequences from the action that you are about to take. It's the kind of instinct you have to possess to beat guys such as Abdu. I went for the gap but it was so tight that I knocked off about half a dozen wing mirrors from the line of cars as my right hand hit them as I sprinted clear of the pack. Each time I hit one of the mirrors it would jam on the brakes.

But I was away and no-one, not even a rider as fast and strong as Abdoujaparov could catch me. It was no fluke in that race as I beat Abdu again on the final stage in Westminster. It was a circuit race that finished on Vauxhall Bridge and on the final lap I had a good lead out from my teammates Mickel Markesson and Alan Dippen. As we left Fleet Street the barriers narrowed as we came onto Vauxhall Bridge, as we were only racing on one half of the road, with the other half still open to traffic. I was the first to launch my sprint and so got the advantage on everyone else. Abdoujaparov was right behind me and he tried to get past on the inside between me and barriers, but as the road narrowed it was too tight for him to get through. I could hear his brake lever clinking on the metal barrier as he tried to force his way through, but in the end even he decided it was too dangerous, braked, and then switched to try and pass me on the outside. I had held my line as sprinters are supposed to do; it was the fact that the line of barriers came out into the road and narrowed the finish that forced Abdu to brake. I hadn't moved, but he didn't see it that way and we ended up fighting after the finish surrounded by a huge crowd of press, spectators, riders and team helpers. Abdu claiming that I had tried to put him in the barriers was ironic when in subsequent years he zigzagged his way to wins on the Continent with many of his rivals protesting to the commissaries about his sprinting. Abdu seemed to think it was okay to bounce from one side of the road to the other in a sprint, but he didn't like it if he got beat.

There's no doubt he was fast, but he won more races than he should have done because there were times when he should have been disqualified for not holding his line in a sprint. But he was ruthless, and I suppose his tough background growing up behind the Iron Curtain had a lot to do with that. His cycling ability gave him a chance to escape from that regime and he was determined to make the most of that opportunity and was quite literally not going to let anyone get in his way. His career came to an end after a positive dope test; he tested positive more than once during his career. Maybe another indicator of his ruthless and single-minded desire to win at any cost.

For riders such as Abdu, and for that matter many other Soviet Bloc riders of that era, every race was a matter of life or death. You only have to watch the madness of the 1991 Tour de France sprint on the Champs Elysees to see that; Abdu, riding with his head down, zigzagging all over the road and then ploughing into the barriers at 45mph causing a mass pile-up. He was a bloody mess, but he got up and crossed the line to claim the green jersey and the prize money. I don't think he cared too much about the rules of cycling, he just saw the sport as a way of escaping the hard life he would have had back in Tashkent had he not been able to make money from racing. But racing against him, and beating him, proved that once I got the jump on other riders in a sprint, even if they were as fast as The Tashkent Tornado, it was very rare for anyone to come past me in those final metres to the line. Once I had my sprinting blinkers on and couldn't see anyone either side of me, and only the finish line in front, the race was usually mine. When I look at what he went on to achieve just a few years later it does make me wonder about how much ability I had and whether I could have been good enough to win big continental races. Beating Kelly, Roche, Anderson and Abdoujaparov at various stages of my career also makes me wonder about what might have been when I look at the record books and see what they achieved.

When I look back at how my career compared with Abdu's, it also makes me think about the drugs issue and whether I would have been asked to cheat if I had gone to a continental team. Certainly in the 1980s, I believe it was very difficult for any rider to be competitive without taking drugs in the big tours. I'm not saying that everyone who raced on the Continent was on drugs, as there were exceptions. But there is enough proof around that many were cheating; you only have to look at the list of those who have either tested positive for performance enhancing drugs or who have admitted to doping. Only recently Steven Rooks and Laurent Fignon, two guys I raced against, have admitted to doping. There are many more. I don't know whether Abdu was on something when I raced against him but he did get caught cheating later in his career.

Performance enhancing drugs were offered to me during my racing days but I turned them down. I knew other guys were doping; I spoke to a few riders from Eastern Bloc countries who told me that they were on steroids and growth hormones among other things. I'm glad that I didn't cheat, because I can now look back on what I won and know that my conscience is clear. Everything I achieved was down to a mixture of talent and hard work. I was able to win races without cheating while I knew some riders who were taking drugs just to get to the finish in races. Maybe I would have won more if I had taken something and I admit there were times when I felt envious if I was beaten by a rider who I was sure was taking drugs. But I knew that if I did take something that I would probably get caught; just as I used to get caught when breaking the rules as a kid at school, I knew that if anyone was going to get caught cheating by taking drugs, it would be Steve Joughin. Everything that I had ever won would instantly be tainted. I'd made a name for myself in the UK and even more so in the Isle of Man. If I had tested positive for something it would have been splashed across all the newspapers in the Island and I just couldn't bear the thought of putting myself and my family through that.

I'm glad to see that cycling has made more of an effort to confront the doping issue in recent years, and certainly cycling has done more to catch cheats than sports such as football or tennis. But there will always be riders who get away with it. There will always be doctors around who are one step ahead of the drug testers, so it is a battle that will just go on and on. People cheat in all walks of life and professional cycling is no different. No matter how difficult it becomes to beat the dope testers there will always be someone who thinks they are smart enough to cheat and get away with it. Even now, if a sports doctor came along offering a drug that would guarantee to put a rider way ahead of everyone else and was undetectable - but might kill you before your 50th birthday - a lot of riders would still take that chance in order to achieve success. That's human nature. When it comes to rivalry in cycling, the biggest one of all is often with the rider's own character, and it is that which determines whether they try to win within the rules or win at any cost.

Every competitor in every sport has to make their own decision about doping. I chose not to cheat and I'm glad that I made that choice. But what I didn't realise when I was racing was that I already had an addiction. It wasn't to doping or to drugs of any kind. I was addicted to winning, addicted to the buzz that I got from that moment of elation when I crossed the line with my arms in the air and heard the crowd cheering. In all my years of racing I never gave a thought to what life might be like when those moments were gone forever. I guess when you are young you don't think too much about the future. It was only when I retired from racing that I realised just how much the sport meant to me and how I had relied for so many years on that winning feeling to give me a buzz and boost my confidence. When the time came to hang up my wheels and retire from racing I had to find something else to replace that high, and that search was to bring my world crashing down around me.

STAGE 9
End of the road

In 2005 I lay in a hospital room in Italy, strapped to the bed to prevent me thrashing around due to suffering delirium tremens - the DTs - a classic sign of someone with a serious alcohol problem. For years I had managed to persuade myself that I didn't have a drink problem; mentally I'd managed to find a way of justifying my continuing reliance on alcohol. But after a business trip to Italy my body finally began to break down. This was the lowest point in my battle with drink, but it had all begun many years earlier.

As a full-time bike rider you have to watch what you eat and drink. It's just not possible to have a drink problem and hope to have a successful career. During my time as rider I had the occasional blow out and would get drunk to drown my sorrows after losing a race or to celebrate a victory. I remember one occasion when my wife Joanne was expecting our first child, Ben. It was the evening of the Kellogg's City Centre Series race in Glasgow on August 18, 1986. Going into the final corner I was perfectly placed and felt that I was going to win, but as I rounded the corner my pedal caught the front wheel of the Australian Danny Clark. Instead of using the traditional clips and strap type pedals I was using one of the first clipless pedal designs. It was an Adidas version that never caught on and what happened to me next is one of the reasons why. The pedals had a lever on the outside that you moved in order to release your foot. The lever caught in Clarke's wheel and, as I launched my sprint, my foot came out of the pedal. I slowed and got my foot back in but it came out again and eventually I had to settle for fourth.

Frustrated at losing the race and feeling low, I went out on the town with Mike Doyle, my mate from the Isle of Man who was also riding in the race. We decided to show Glasgow what it meant to have a good night out and we both ended up bladdered. Back at the hotel at 2.00am the phone went and it was my mother-in-law, who said that Joanne had gone into labour in Stoke-on-Trent and that Ben would be born in the next few hours. I didn't know what to do, but when I woke Sid Barras, our team captain, he said that if it was him in the same situation he would go straight to the hospital. The problem was that Doyler and I were still recovering from the night before. By the time I returned to my hotel room, Doyler had packed our bags. I looked at him and said: 'What are you doing?'

'We're going mate,' he said. And so we put our bags in a Ford Granada and headed for the Potteries. Around two hours later we arrived in Stoke. In the end we needn't have rushed as Ben wasn't born until 10.00am, but the story shows that alcohol was part of my life while I was racing, even if such episodes were rare.

During my racing career I wasn't addicted to alcohol. What I was addicted to was racing and winning. It was like a drug and it was only when I retired from racing that I realised that I had been hooked ever since I began racing as a kid. Whenever I lost a race, particularly when it was one that I knew I should have won, I would be down in the dumps until I won again. Maybe that was a sign of an addictive personality. I needed to win to satisfy that side of my character. Sometimes when I had a bad result because I was over-trained and tired I used to do the wrong thing. If I had lost a race that I'd wanted to win, I would sometimes go out and train even harder than before. Even if I was fatigued from a race or a period of heavy training, I'd go out and cane myself because I was so desperate to win the next time. The adrenalin buzz of racing, and in particular the danger and speed of a bunch sprint, was something I craved as soon as I hung up my wheels up and retired in 1991 at the age of thirty-two. It had been a difficult decision to make, but in the end I felt that it was time to move on, as a lot of sponsors had pulled out of the sport in the UK. I had a mortgage and bills to pay and I felt that there wasn't enough money for me in racing anymore.

Towards the end of my career I really hated training and dreaded having to do four or five-hour training rides. The winter breaks seemed to get shorter and shorter. When fatigue sets in at the end of a long season all pro riders look forward to having a break, but those winter months seemed to go so quickly in the last few years of my pro career. I used to hammer the gym, doing weights in the winter because it was much more difficult to get back in shape if I had too much of a rest in the off-season. That meant that it didn't feel like I was getting much of a break from training but I knew that I had to do it. I knew that much of my sprinting ability came from the power and strength I developed in the gym, and upper body strength was as important as having big leg muscles so I did hours and hours of weights, circuit training and running in the winter.

After eight years of being a pro – eight years of being constantly on the road and spending so much time living out of a suitcase in hotel rooms, away from my wife and family – the lifestyle was starting to get me down.

The final straw came when the team I was riding for, KGC Carpets, decided to withdraw its sponsorship, with the deal ending two days before the national road race. During my pro career I'd never finished outside the top 10 in the national road race so it seemed unfair to end the contract, particularly so close to the race. That made my mind up and I decided to retire.

Suddenly, it was all over. The lifestyle that I had led since I was a teenager was gone. For the best part of twenty years every day had been dedicated to training and racing, to making myself a better cyclist. Now, without any fanfare, it was finished. Nothing really prepared me for how that sudden change might affect me.

I went back to college and did a course in leisure and recreation and got a job as a sports supervisor at a leisure centre in Cannock, Staffordshire. Then I started to run my own mountain bike training schools for kids and also organised some races. Then I moved into the cycle business, selling Cougar bikes and in 1998 I went into the cycle clothing business with my own company, ProVision, which I still run today with my son, Ben. I didn't find it difficult to make a living after retiring from racing; what I found difficult was living without that buzz from racing and winning. Crossing the finish line at the end of a race, punching my arms in air and hearing the crowd cheer was something that just couldn't be replaced when I retired.

The need to have a disciplined lifestyle with regard to eating and drinking was also gone. I didn't have to spend hours training every day, and found that I spent more and more time socialising, which usually happened in the local pub. I became what is known as a functioning alcoholic. I didn't realise it at the time, but I was becoming increasingly reliant on drink, but everything seemed okay because I was able to work normally and, initially at least, alcohol wasn't causing me any problems.

As time passed the feeling of missing the emotional high I got from racing and the pressure of business started to get to me and sent me into a deep depression. Alcoholism is a progressive illness; it doesn't just happen overnight, but instead creeps up on you over months and years. When it became apparent that I had a problem my friends would tell me that I must be able to beat the illness. As a rider I was determined and, as all pro riders do, I had an ability to drive myself to achieve many things if I put my mind to them. But this was something I couldn't beat on my own, no matter how hard I tried. I was very rarely drunk but instead would need to constantly top up my alcohol level during the day. I very often got into my car while over the limit but was never stopped by the police. I went to Alcoholics Anonymous in 2003 and was told how the illness would progress. But I carried on drinking.

By 2005 I knew that my drinking was out of control but I was still managing to work and to conceal the extent of the problem from my family. In the mornings I would wake up shaking due to being asleep and without having a drink for eight hours. When Joanne and the kids started to suspect that I had a problem, they urged me to stop. My response to this was to go underground and I began to hide booze around the house so I could have a drink without anyone knowing.

That year I went on a business trip to Italy and on the way to the airport I got two bottles of water. One I emptied and filled with vodka, the other I kept to give to the person I was meeting just in case they asked for a sip of my water and got a surprise. I had to sip the vodka constantly because by this stage I was getting withdrawal symptoms if I didn't. When my alcohol level dropped I would start to shake and sweat – classic sign of the DTs. On my second day in Italy I had another meeting, but in the morning I didn't have a drink. By the afternoon I was getting severe withdrawal symptoms. But this time it was different. The sweating and shaking was getting out of control, and then I had an epileptic fit brought on by my body's dependence on alcohol. The seizure was so severe that I almost bit my tongue in two and snapped off a few teeth as my jaw snapped shut.

In hospital I was strapped down while the doctors put drips into my arm. I was kept in for a week on high doses of valium. Joanne came out to see me; there was no point pretending that I didn't have a serious problem anymore. I was lucky to be alive and, after such a dramatic wake-up call, you would think that would be enough of a shock to make me realise that I had to stop drinking. But what happened next shows just how addictive alcohol can be.

After a week in hospital in Italy, and after putting my wife and family through days of worry, I arrived back home in Stoke-on-Trent. As soon as I got back home I went straight to the off-licence. That was the madness of what I was going through. Even after cheating death only a few days before, I still wanted to drink. My addiction to alcohol continued, despite the knowledge of what it was doing to my health and my family. Later in 2005 Joanne dragged me to an alcohol treatment clinic in Stoke-on-Trent called the Edward Myers Centre. I was treated alongside alcoholics and with drug addicts, some of whom were hooked on heroine. I was put on a high dosage course of diazepam, a kind of sedative that helped lessen the withdrawal symptoms I would usually experience when my body was deprived of alcohol. I was given high dose injections of a vitamin B complex which also helped to minimise the withdrawal symptoms. I was locked in there while the treatment took effect and to prevent me from being tempted to take a drink.

After four weeks in the Edward Myers Centre I had dried out and stayed sober all over Christmas and New Year, a time feared by alcoholics, as it's expected that everyone should have a drink to celebrate. But I got through it and was still dry in February. I felt that I had done well and that I had finally conquered my addiction. Fear of going back to all the problems I had suffered due to drink stopped me from falling into my old bad habits for a while. But as time passed I got complacent, and that's a dangerous thing for anyone with a drink problem; you are only ever one drink away from falling back into grip of addiction. After two months dry, I thought it would be fine to have one drink without becoming hooked again. I walked into my local pub and had a pint of lager. I thought I could have a drink like anyone who doesn't have an alcohol problem. I got away with it. I had one pint then went home. No problem.

A few days later it was beautifully sunny, the kind of day when it's great to sit outside having a cold drink in the sunshine. By this time I thought that the problem I had was just a blip and that I could have a few drinks and not get addicted again. So I went and had another couple of drinks in the sunshine. Within two weeks I was back on the treadmill of drinking first thing in the morning and had fallen into the grip of my addiction once again. Even if I stopped drinking for an hour or two, I would start shaking and sweating just like before. In a way, it was now worse because I knew how difficult it had been for me to stop drinking and I had the memory of how awful it was going to be if I tried to stop again. It sounds crazy, but I was more scared of stopping drinking than I was of dying.

Eventually, I ended up back at the Edward Myers Centre and when I came out this time I had learnt my lesson and realised that it wasn't safe for me to drink at all. I went to Alcoholics Anonymous and listened to all of the issues faced by others with drink problems. I listened to what AA members call the 'yet' stories. I'd hear someone tell a horror story, such as crashing their car while drunk and think to myself: 'Well, at least I haven't done anything as bad as that'. For AA members, the tag line to that thought is: 'You mean you haven't done anything as bad as that *yet*.'

At one time I'd heard stories about alcoholics crashing their cars while drunk and had thought that I would never do that. But I had ended up doing exactly that. I'd thought my drinking would never cause problems at home but there were times when I smashed the house up while drunk. Almost all of the 'yet' stories I heard at AA meetings, and dismissed as things that would never happen to me, eventually came true. It's an example of how the illness creeps up on you. When I initially contacted AA and went to meetings I thought that I would never end up like so many of the members I listened to. But I did end up that way. Hearing all these horror stories didn't prevent me from going through the same experiences, but it did show that my addiction really was beyond my control and that I needed help.

In the end I went through the AA 12-step programme and haven't had a drink now since September 19, 2006. AA has helped me get my life back on track and now I do voluntary work for the group, helping others face the demons that I have had to come to terms with. I now put as much effort into helping those with drink problems as I do into my own business. It's my way of thanking those at AA who helped me. If my alcohol addiction had continued unchecked, I would have lost everything; my family, my business – maybe even my life.

My good friend and former teammate Mike Doyle also had to overcome a drink problem when he finished racing and there are many other sports stars who have had similar problems – George Best, Tony Adams, Paul Merson and Marco Pantani, to name but a few who have battled addiction at varying stages of their careers.

Thierry Claveyrolat, who was born in the same year as me and won the King of the Mountains prize in the Tour de France, committed suicide a few years after he retired from racing despite having a successful business and winning the French lottery. He developed a drink problem and was involved in a road accident in which a family had been seriously hurt. He took his own life a few weeks later.

Mark Bell from Liverpool was a rider I raced against many times during my career and everyone involved in cycling was shocked when he died in 2009. Mark could be a brilliant rider on his day, but he had constant battles with demons that drove him to drink and it was the effects of alcoholism which eventually led to his untimely death.

Even when a rider appears to have it all, and seems to be living the dream of being a pro cyclist, they can still suffer bouts of depression that often lead to drink problems. When Bradley Wiggins won three medals at the Athens Olympics, who would have suspected that he would go home and sink into a deep depression which would lead to periods of heavy drinking? But that's exactly what happened to him, and the experiences he details in his autobiography show that even a rider at the very top of his game is at risk once the cheers die down and the euphoria of victory fades in the weeks and months after the medal ceremony. Tom Boonen, a former World Road Race Champion and prolific classics winner, had his own addiction problems. There are many more riders who have faced similar demons.

Maybe there is something about dedicating your life to excellence in one particular field that means you are more prone to an addiction or depression once you retire. Certainly in cycling you have to be obsessive about training and racing to be a success. At least being obsessive about sporting excellence is something positive, but for some that obsessive nature and the constant need for success can have a darker side which I found out to my cost.

When I was racing, it curbed my desire to drink and the demands of being a cyclist acted as a controlling mechanism for my drinking. I didn't realise it at the time, but cycling was a healthy addiction that was preventing me from falling into an unhealthy one. It was only when I stopped racing, and this controlling mechanism was taken away, that my problems with alcohol really began. I was lucky in that I had the support of my wife, Joanne, and my two sons, who stuck by me despite what I put them through. Joanne and the kids had to stand and watch me spinning out of control. It was like someone throwing a stone into a pond and watching the ripples spreading out across the water. And all of the ripples are those that are affected; alcoholism affects everyone in that person's life. Cyclists have to be selfish in order to be successful and their attention is mostly on themselves and what they need to do to win races. So Joanne had to put up with all of that side of my character too.

Joanne was at her wits end sometimes, not knowing what more she could do to help. She had moved with me from the Island to England when she was just eighteen and stuck by my side as I tried to make it as a pro. When I did turn pro, I was away for months at a time racing while she was at home raising Ben. Then I put her through all the trauma of struggling to overcome my drink problem. I'm so lucky that she has always stood by me; I've put her through some tough times. I'm not proud of it, and I appreciate her always being there to help me through. Having her support and the experiences that we have both gone through during my battle against alcoholism has brought us even closer together.

My family tried to help as much as they could and knowing that they were standing by me helped me to get through it. But in the end it was down to me to want to help myself. I think I was lucky in that I hadn't made enough money from racing to retire on. I had to carry on working and this helped; knowing that I had to make a living to look after my family was something that drove me on to get through my problems. I knew that if I carried on drinking I would lose everything and that I wouldn't be able to support my family. If I'd had enough in the bank to retire on I might still be drinking now. I would have ended up like Paul Gascoigne, the former England footballer. If you have enough money to live on for the rest of your life, then you are less likely to run into financial problems that will affect you as a consequence of drinking too much.

One of my inspirations for writing this book is the hope that it may be of some help to anyone reading it who is struggling with alcohol addiction. There were times when I felt that the only way I could escape from my drink dependency was to kill myself. Sometimes I would be driving and thinking that if I just turned the wheel to the right, I could drive head on into a truck and it would all be over. That seemed the only way out at times, but I was lucky in that I received help in time. AA can help and I would urge anyone with a drink problem to pick up the phone and call them sooner rather than later. I still have to be aware of not falling back into bad habits, but right now I'm enjoying life more than I have ever done. Even someone in the very deepest grip of alcoholism can find a way out, if they get help. I'm living proof of that.

Now I do voluntary work for AA using my experiences to help others cope with their own problems. It means a lot to me to give something back to AA which has helped me get my life back on track.

If you are reading this and thinking that my story resembles your own experience, then make that call now. It could be the start of your own journey back to health and, believe me, it is a journey worth making. I won't tell you how good the end of that journey will be, you can make that discovery for yourself. In the UK you can call 0845 769 7555 or go to www.alcoholics-anonymous.org.uk

STAGE 10
Hiding in the wheels

When you watch cycling on TV today you can get high definition images, cameras on motorbikes and helicopters and even some on the bikes of the riders themselves. There's any number of interviews during the race with team managers and ex-riders and loads of chat with the riders as soon as they have crossed the finish line. It's great for fans to have access to all of this detail but, apart from the Tour de France, a lot of media coverage only scratches the surface of what happens in a big race.

Any rider who has been in a major race will tell you that there are so many stories, so many incidents and so many different emotions that it's impossible to convey all of that on TV or in the press. There's so much that is hidden, not least the emotional rollercoaster experienced by pro riders racing day after day, season after season. To be a professional cyclist requires a certain mindset because you have to get into a routine of racing, eating and sleeping day in, day out. That routine takes over your life to the point where it feels that there is nothing else going on in the world other than the race you are in. Some riders can't deal with that mentally, even though they may have the physical ability to cope with it. But if you can cope, it is a fantastic experience and one that can becomes addictive. It's the reason why you see so many ex-pros involved as team managers, mechanics or drivers. Even after a decade or more living out of a suitcase during their racing careers, some miss the buzz and the camaraderie of racing so much that they have to go back for more.

Stage races in particular are full of incidents that only those involved in the race can really share or truly understand. Racing day after day for two or three weeks is something you really have to do if you are to truly appreciate what it is like; the emotional highs and lows, the friendships and quarrels, the acts of selflessness by teammates and the moments of betrayal. A stage race is a soap opera on wheels and, even with the blanket media coverage of big races, only a fraction of what happens behind the scenes ever gets reported.

Stage races require riders to have a certain mentality too. Even if a rider has the physical ability to cope, they may not have that mental strength. As Lance Armstrong says: 'Stage racing is as tough on the mind as it is on the legs.' Anyone who has ridden a big stage race would agree with those words.

One of the things that helps you survive stage races is having a good team and lots of mates you can turn to when the going gets tough. No matter how good you are, a rider will always need to turn to someone for help at times and it's certainly true that a rider who makes enemies in the peloton will find it much harder to win. If someone unpopular is in a breakaway, there will be no shortage of volunteers wanting to drive the pace at the front.

Another aspect of racing that can only really be appreciated by those who have raced at pro level is the amount of hard work that goes into winning races. Training day after day is hard, mentally and physically. It may seem a bit bizarre but I never had a coach to advise me on training, I just learned as I went along. I tried to pick up advice from experienced riders such as Barry Hoban, but for the most part my training schedule was devised by trial and error. Over the years I got to know what worked for me and what didn't. From the age of around fifteen I was constantly talking to more experienced riders and asking them questions and I believe this inquisitiveness and desire to learn helped me to develop as a rider. Right through my career I never missed an opportunity to pick the brains of anyone I could learn from.

I remember training with guys such as John Herety, Paul Sherwen and Graham Jones and they would regularly do rides of five and six hours. A lot of the time I'd just join them for a couple of hours in the morning then go home, get showered, have something to eat and then sleep. In the evening I'd train again but would do a shorter, more intense, session behind a car or motorbike. This combination of an endurance ride and speed training split into two sessions worked well for me. It's something that a lot of riders do now, so even though I had a trial and error approach to training there were some things that I hit upon that worked even though I didn't have a coach. However, with the benefit of hindsight, not having a coach or a mentor was a mistake, but I just did what I thought was right at the time.

When it came to bikes and equipment I was always a stickler for attention to detail. Some of that was forced upon me by being only five feet three inches tall. It wasn't easy to find a frame small enough to fit me, so I got most of my custom-made by Brian Rourke in Stoke-on-Trent. Brian is a respected frame builder and has supplied bikes to many elite riders, his most famous customer in recent years being the World and Olympic road race champion Nicole Cooke.

I had a range of bikes built for long road races and for criteriums. The criterium bike would have a top tube an inch longer than my normal road bike so that I could stretch out more and get lower on the bike, which made me a bit more aerodynamic and gave me a lower centre of gravity which was useful when racing round tight corners at speed. The criterium machine would have shorter cranks and a higher bottom bracket so that I could pedal through corners better than on the road bike.

There were other details that I was very finicky about. I always had to have Cinelli 65 handlebars, which a lot of sprinters liked because they allowed for a comfortable hand position when sprinting out of the saddle. Handlebar tape had to be the old cotton type; I hated the plastic stuff that appeared in the 1980s as you couldn't get good grip on it when your hands began to sweat. I hated wearing track mitts too. Even though the palms of my hands would get ripped to pieces if I crashed, I still liked to race without anything between my hands and the handlebars so I could get the best grip.

My bikes always had to be immaculate and as kid I spent hours polishing the old steel rims with Duraglit to get a mirror finish good enough to shave in. One of the benefits of working in the bus garage as a teenager was that I could boil my bike chain in oil to get it perfectly clean.

That was the sort of obsessive nature I had and one that many former pro riders will recognise. Cycling is such a demanding sport that it consumes your life; to an extent it has to if you are to fulfil your potential. It's still the same today and I admire Mark Cavendish for the way in which he and his team prepare so well for races and win so consistently, even though all the other teams know exactly what to expect when the race comes down to a bunch sprint. Cav is incredibly fast, but that's only one of the talents that make him successful.

The thing that really impresses me about him is his ability to cope with the pressure of being the fastest man in road racing, dealing with all the media hype and the knowledge that his teammates sacrifice their own chances to work for him. But Mark is the sort of character that is motivated more by the pressure he puts on himself than by the pressure from his team or the media.

Coping with that sort of pressure was always something I struggled with, and I couldn't adapt to living abroad so never got the chance to compete in the big continental races that Mark has been so successful in. As a Manxman, I am so proud when I see him winning stages in the Tour de France or the Milan-San Remo. He doesn't need advice from me on how to win or handle the challenges that he will meet as his career develops. But one thing I have talked to him about, though, is to savour every moment and every victory because his career will flash by in the blink of an eye.

When you are winning races regularly it can feel as though there will always be another victory, so it can come as a shock when it is all over. Pro bike racing gave me a chance to make a living doing something that I loved. I realise that I was very lucky to have that opportunity. The boom in racing in the UK in the 1980s gave a lot of riders a chance to turn pro, an opportunity that they wouldn't have had in the UK in earlier years. Okay, we weren't making a lot of money compared with footballers or continental pro riders, but it was better than working down a coal mine or in a factory. Even a five-hour training ride in the freezing rain is better than working nine to five.

Over the past few years I've had to forget the major achievements I had in cycling and concentrate on the here and now, one day at a time. As part of that process I've started to enjoy riding my bike again. That's meant having to forget about how I used to approach sport and the time in my life when cycling meant racing to win. And winning meant everything. Now I'm rediscovering the same enthusiasm I had for cycling as a 14-year-old, when I just wanted to ride my bike and the only thing that upset me was when it rained on a Sunday and there was no club run for me to join in with. The difference now, at the age of 51, is that I am learning to enjoy cycling without worrying about how slow I am going up hills. That sort of thing doesn't frustrate me now, even if I get passed by other riders. I just remind myself that I'm not in my twenties anymore.

It took me a long time to come to terms with not racing. Even a decade after retiring I was still struggling to cope with a life without that regular adrenaline rush. For years, riding my bike was simply about winning and to prove myself over and over again. I'm glad to say that I'm now happy with life and content with what I achieved as a rider, and can now ride my bike with that same sense of fun and pure enjoyment of cycling I enjoyed all those years ago.

STAGE 11
Pocket Guides
by Richard Allen

In the next few pages you can read interviews with some expert guides to the Pocket Rocket, including those who raced with and against him and the commentators who were behind the mic calling some of his biggest victories. We start with my own memories:

My obsession with cycling began when I was a bored teenager in the West Midlands in England, sat at home one Monday evening in late summer flicking channels on the TV. I was a football fan at a loose end during the off-season. We only had four TV channels to choose from back then so it didn't take long to flick through them all. I happened to switch on to Channel 4's Kellogg's City Centre Cycling series and watched an action-packed hour-long show of crashes and controversy.

I'd watched some brief Tour de France highlights on World of Sport but never really understood the event or its history. Despite being an avid sports fan, cycling had never really captured my imagination. When I began watching the city centre series I couldn't even ride a bike, but after a few weeks of watching races I was hooked and suddenly I wanted to learn to ride and learn more about this sport of cycle racing which had so far passed me by. Those Kellogg's-sponsored races inspired my interest in cycling. I'm sure there are many more cycling fans out there who were inspired to take up the sport via the same route.

It was fast and furious racing, and winning and losing seemed to be a matter of life and death to some of the riders. What made it even more interesting for me was the contrast in characters; the continental riders, with superstar status, against the rather more gritty UK professionals. Phil Anderson seemed to epitomise the glamour of pro cycling and the gutsy, never-say-die attitude you had to have to be a winner. As a cricket fan, when I first saw Anderson racing in the Kelloggs series, I thought it was Jeff Thompson on a bike. He was all blond hair, sun tan and he had more teeth than a Great White - and the killer instinct to match. Next to him and the other continental stars such as Roche and Moser, some of the UK pros looked to be on a hiding to nothing.

Steve Joughin stood out for obvious reasons. He was always the smallest rider in the race. Phil Thomas appeared to be a character who had wondered across from Channel 4's Liverpool-based soap opera Brookside, while Sid Barras, then the elder statesman of the UK pro scene, was in the final flourish of his long career.

I looked at the line-ups on the start line and it seemed like Real Madrid were about to take on Accrington Stanley. It appeared to me to be a David versus Goliath contest - plucky British pros against their more highly-paid and more famous continental rivals who were stars of the Tour de France. But that preconception of it being an unequal contest all changed once the racing started.

Thomas was a match for anyone in the Kellogg's criteriums, a tactical master who infuriated the continentals with some of his, shall we say, fearless riding on the tight city centre circuits. And there was Malcolm Elliott, the Sheffield sprinter, who would go on to have a successful continental career and who appeared to win races without ever breaking sweat. He made it look that easy. Then there was Keith 'Legs' Lambert and Phil 'Staffordshire Engine' Bayton who powered around the criterium circuits as if they were on motorbikes. 'Super' Sid Barras belied his years with displays of pure guts and determination and proved that his legs could match those of riders ten years his junior. I always used to wonder if there was some rule in British cycling that said you could only have a pro licence if you had a nickname. Of course, the man with the best nickname of them all was the 'Pocket Rocket' himself. As a convert to cycling I quickly got used to looking for the little man from the Isle of Man in the bunch sprints as Joughin fired himself out of the peloton like a cork out of a champagne bottle.

I was in Birmingham on the day that Steve won a stage of the Kellogg's Pro Tour of Britain in 1987. A great ride in a race that had a top-class field, including Sean Kelly and Steven Rooks. I remembered Steve primarily as a sprinter and it was only when I met him fifteen years after he retired, and wrote a Cycling Weekly feature about him, that I realised he was much more of an all-rounder than I had thought, and looking at some of the scalps he took during his career he may well have been good enough to win continental races had he been able to adapt to living abroad.

Being asked to write a book about a rider who had been a star of a racing series that inspired my passion for cycling has been a real pleasure and a privilege. Researching this book has been like a long stroll down memory lane, looking back at what I consider a golden age of British cycling. I hope I've helped Steve do his story justice.

One thing that occurred to me in researching this book is just how many talented riders Britain had in the 1980s. Robert Millar, Sean Yates, Malcolm Elliott, Paul Sherwen, Graham Jones, John Herety, Joey McLoughlin, Adrian Timmis, Paul Watson, Sid Barras, Phil Thomas, Nigel Dean, Tim Harris, Rob Holden, Phil Bayton, Chris Walker, Keith Reynolds, Darryl Webster, Steve Jones, Chris Lillywhite, Tony Doyle, Mike Doyle and, of course, Steve Joughin. All of them had successful careers, whether based on the Continent or in the UK. But I can't help wondering just how much more they would have achieved had they been given the support that is now available to riders via British Cycling.

There's no doubt that had cycling in Britain been structured as it is today with National Lottery funded programmes, we would have seen a greater number of those names listed above winning big continental races. Now, if a British rider has the talent and is prepared to work hard, there are no barriers to success in continental racing. In the 1980s there was no funding, no Olympic Academy programmes, no British-based superteams such as Team Sky. A rider with the ability to win the Tour de France would be much better off being from France or Spain rather than Britain.

The thoughts of what might have been may have put a small cloud over British racing in the 1980s, but the silver lining is that the lack of opportunities to make it in continental racing meant that most of Britain's (and the Isle of Man's) talented riders spent the majority of their careers racing on British roads. And that was to the benefit of all those cycling fans who enjoyed some of the most exciting and inspiring road racing that Britain has ever seen.

Mike Doyle

Isle of Man cyclist who was a pro rider with Moducel, PMS-Dawes and ANC-Interrent teams in the 1980s. He is now coach for Team Isle of Man-Microgaming, the Island's national cycling team:

Mike Doyle grew up in the Isle of Man and when he started racing 'Jockey' was competing in the same junior events at King George V Park in Douglas, although he was a couple of years older. Right from the start Doyle says it was obvious that Joughin had a great sprint.

'When he went and won the Merseyside Division title as a junior it made many people take notice of him because at that time most of the UK's top riders were from that region,' says Mike. 'Anyone who won the Merseyside Division title was automatically a favourite to win the national title. When he won the British national junior series too, it inspired a lot of riders in the Isle of Man. Ron Killey, who coached me and Jockey, told me that I could follow in Steve's footsteps and this inspired me to get out and train harder. I won the national junior series too, a year after Steve had won it, so he had a positive effect on my career. Having someone I knew as a friend and club mate achieving great things in junior racing really gave me a sense of possibility and boosted my confidence. '

In later years both Mike and Steve raced in France.

'It was an adventure for us, two lads from a small island competing on the Continent against some of the best riders in the world, including Fignon, Roche and Anderson,' says Mike. 'I'd gone to race in France as a 19-year-old and Jockey joined me after I'd spent a year out there and got a few decent results. If we were racing now we'd probably have been on the GB programme but back in the eighties it was a case of fending for yourself and making your own way through the amateur ranks and then turning pro if you were given the chance. Everything was done on a wing and a prayer. Me and Jockey used to hitch lifts in cargo planes from the Isle of Man to Ireland in order to save money to get to races. There were times when we'd sit freezing cold in the back of the plane with nothing but our bikes, kit bags and a few thousand frozen beefburgers for company; many a time we'd arrive on the start line of a race with our clothes still stinking of burgers, fish fingers or whatever the cargo plane happened to be carrying that week.

'But trips like that were worth it, not just because it was a great laugh, but because we'd often clean up all the prizes in criteriums. If we were lucky we'd get prize money, but we might end up with anything from frozen chickens to gas cookers.'

Mike recalls that Steve was never a man to let bizarre prizes get in the way of him saving a few bob here and there: 'When we won half a dozen gas cookers at one race in Ireland neither hell nor high water - or a fifty-mile trip across the Irish Sea back to the Isle of Man – was going to get in the way of him saving a few quid and getting them back to the Island.'

Stories such as that typify the kind of adventures the Manx duo had during their racing careers and they are still telling and re-telling them long after they hung up their wheels.

'Whenever we get together with other ex-pros from the 1980s all of these stories come out and we end up reliving races won and lost two decades ago,' says Mike. 'Telling those

159

stories makes my legs ache more now than it did when I was racing. Jockey was a brilliant rider and had a great career. On his day he was match for anyone in a sprint. I believe he could have been successful with a big continental team but he never felt at home when we went to France.

'He was only there for a few months and he won races but he never took to the French way of life or the regimented life that we had to lead to try and make it with a pro team. I think if Jockey had gone to the Continent a few years earlier, he may have been able to adapt to it. He was twenty-one by the time he went to France with me and I think that by then he had become used to racing in England and the pattern of the season. Barry Hoban always advised riders to go to the Continent as early as possible so that young riders got used to the continental way of life and way of racing as soon as possible.

'It's easy to say with hindsight, but Jockey gave continental racing his best shot and in the end it just wasn't for him. But physically he was good enough to win stages of the Tour de France and maybe classics too, as his record of beating the likes of Kelly, Abdoujaprov and Roche proves.'

Phil Liggett

For more than thirty years Phil Liggett has been the voice of the Tour de France for cycling fans in the English-speaking world. As well as being a journalist and commentator, Phil was also the organiser of the Milk Race in Great Britain for many years, a race which saw the emergence of a brash young sprinter from the Isle of Man in the 1980s. Liggett commentated on many of Steve Joughin's greatest moments on the bike and it is he who Joughin credits with giving him his 'Pocket Rocket' nickname:

As race organiser of the Milk Race, Phil Liggett was only too pleased when British riders came along to break the domination of the Soviet Union. A British, or Isle of Man, victory meant the UK press would give more coverage to the event, which kept sponsors happy and helped secure the future of the race. In 1981 there had been a few years with little to cheer for the home nation's riders in the Milk Race. Then, like a cork out of a champagne bottle, up popped a pocket-sized powerhouse called Steve Joughin who won the opening road stage in Bournemouth and took the leader's yellow jersey.

'I don't recall being the first commentator to give Steve his nickname, but I'm delighted if I was the first to call him that,' says Phil. 'It was an appropriate nickname for him. My first real memories of him are from the Milk Race when he won the opening stage in 1981 while racing as an amateur for the Great Britain team. Steve had an explosive sprint, rather like Mark Cavendish does now. Steve was so small you never saw him until the finish. At that time there was a dearth of successes for British riders in the Milk Race, the Russians cleaned up year after year.'

For riders from behind the Iron Curtain winning Milk Race stages meant that they could spend their winnings on goods that they could not get back home. Many Soviet and East German riders would go on spending sprees during the race. Prizes for first place were much greater than for second or third and this, says Phil, meant that the Eastern Bloc riders went all out for victory. He says that in those days race organisers were able to do deals so that the Eastern Bloc riders didn't get hit by excess baggage when they took home goods they bought with their winnings.

'The bikes they rode were absolute wrecks,' says Phil, recalling the machines that Soviet riders turned up to race on. 'But the chains were well-oiled and the tyres were brand new - and the men on the bikes were very tough indeed. When the Pocket Rocket won in 1981 it got the race off to a great start because it meant that a Brit was in yellow and it grabbed the public's imagination and meant that the media would cover the race.'

Phil remembers how the so-called 'Pinta Girls', who presented the prizes on the Milk Race podium, used to tower over Steve. But the little man from the Isle of Man has Phil's gratitude for being good enough to challenge the Soviet domination of the race. 'Steve was a rider who was very necessary for the Milk Race at that time,' he says.

Phil was the commentator for the Kellogg's City Centre Cycling series on Channel 4 and for the Kellogg's Tour of Britain, events which Joughin also had success in. For Phil, the 1980s represented a golden age for cycling in Britain. 'They were halcyon days, the best years for being a professional rider in Britain,' he says. 'I was writing for the Daily Telegraph and the sportsdesk would bite my hand off for race reports and previews because they were impressed with the way the sport was progressing. And Steve Joughin was very much part of it. He was as hard as nails and, although he didn't win a huge number of races, he certainly won some good ones.'

Allan Peiper

Aussie Allan Peiper was one of the most popular riders in the UK in the 1980s even though he raced mostly on the Continent. He was primarily a domestique, working hard for teammates in two of the biggest teams in pro cycling. Allan began his career with Peugeot and then moved on to the Panasonic team, which was one of the most successful in world cycling in the 1980s and was run by Peter Post, one of the greatest team managers of all-time. But he also picked up some big wins, most notably a stage victory in the Giro d'Italia and stage wins in the Nissan Classic Tour of Ireland and Kellogg's Pro Tour of Britain. Allan is now a manager of the HTC-Columbia team:

Allan Peiper's appearances in UK racing were mostly confined to the Kellogg's City Centre Cycling series and the Kellogg's Tour of Britain. He had a lot of success, winning races in Harrogate and Birmingham. In 1987 he became the first rider to win a stage in a professional Tour of Britain when he rode alone into the finish at Newcastle.

He travelled half way around the world to pursue his pro career and the always cheerful Australian won a lot of fans with his aggressive riding style. In the Kellogg's series he was also one of Steve Joughin's main rivals, especially in criteriums.

'Steve's nickname, the Pocket Rocket, says it all,' says Allan. 'He was a fast guy, especially in short races. But mostly I remember Steve as someone who was always light-hearted and friendly, that would be the main memory I have of him.

Steve was a good player in those days and one of the best riders.'

Peiper says that Britain became a home from home for him and he loved racing in the Kellogg's events. 'I turned pro in 1983 and came over to race in the Kellogg's criteriums that year,' he recalls. 'I came over in the car with Paul Sherwen and I just couldn't believe how big the crowds were in Manchester and Birmingham. The races just got bigger and bigger and the criteriums had a good sponsor and it was a real success story. It's what the people wanted to see; short, sharp racing, forty-five minutes of riding and the crowd could see it all in front of them. It was fantastic.

'I went to Belgium to race in 1977 at the age of seventeen and really struggled with homesickness for a few years because I was so young and I didn't have any support from anybody. But when I came to race in Britain I was kind of embraced by the British people and, funnily enough, more so than I was back home in Australia. I really appreciated the support I received and when the Kellogg's Pro Tour of Britain began I considered it as my home race. Even now it means a lot to me to know that I was the first rider to win a stage in the Kellogg's Tour of Britain. It was a great time for racing in the UK.'

'Super' Sid Barras

A pro rider for eighteen years, British road race champion in 1979 and former teammate of Steve Joughin at Moducel in the 1980s. The two are still great mates and Yorkshireman Barras is remembered by many British cycling fans as a competitor and a great sprinter. Barras won a lot of races during his career, but for those fans who began watching cycling on TV in the 1980s he is remembered for his ride on the Newcastle to Manchester stage in the 1987 Kellogg's Tour of Britain when he chased after race leader Steven Rooks in the hills of Yorkshire. Barras, who was riding for the Water Tech-Dawes team that year, was by then the elder statesman of British cycling. The image of Barras being cheered by crowds ten deep on either side of him as he climbed Fleet Moss is one of the enduring images of that golden decade:

Sid Barras had already clocked up fifteen years as a pro rider by the time he joined Steve Joughin in the Moducel team in 1985. Sid was thirty-seven at the time, an age when most pro riders would already have decided to hang up their racing wheels. But joining Moducel gave 'Super' Sid a new lease of life.

'Me and Steve had two good years racing with Moducel in 1985 and 1986,' says Sid. 'They were good years for me and riding in the same team as Steve kind of revived my career. He was young and enthusiastic and a dynamic sprinter.'

But Sid's memories of the Pocket Rocket are not just limited to races when they were teammates. Barras has particular

*In the British champion's jersey and on the wheel of my Moducel team mate
'Super' Sid Barras in a 1985 Kellogg's Criterium*

memories of the 1984 British National Road Race which
Joughin won on home soil in the Isle of Man. 'There were
around seven or eight riders who came around the final
corner together,' says Sid. 'Steve was in the twelve sprocket
and from almost a dead stop launched his sprint and flew
past everyone, including me and Malcolm Elliott. I remember
thinking at time: "Bloody hell, I could sprint like that at one
time!" Steve was just so fast. I've never seen anyone sprint so
fast from a dead stop out of a corner.'

Barras helped Steve win for the team but Steve also
returned the favour and Barras remembers a Kellogg's
criterium in Cardiff in 1985 when the Pocket Rocket acted
as a lead out man for a change, allowing Barras to sprint to
victory.

'Winning that race was a big deal for me as I'd had a poor
year in 1984 and was at the end of my career,' says Sid.

'Riding with Steve revived my career because he was just starting out and was one of the hottest properties in the sport at that time. I didn't want to let him down, and with Mike Doyle and Ian Banbury also riding for Moducel, we had a tremendous team.'

Times change and riders of different eras get different opportunities, with British riders now having many more than those open to British pros in the 1980s. Sid is convinced that if Steve were racing today he would be achieving similar results to the Isle of Man's modern-day cycling hero Mark Cavendish.

'If Jockey was around now he'd be up their sprinting with Cav,' says Sid. 'There's no doubt about it, Steve was a fast lad. I've met Cav a few times and he's a great lad too, and there's no doubt that he is the fastest sprinter in the world right now. Jockey would have been up there with him if he was racing today. But everything is about timing, and you can only do what you can in your own era.'

ACKNOWLEDGEMENTS

With Tour of Britain race director Mick Bennett in 2009. Mick is a former pro rider and was manager of the Ever Ready team when I won my second British Professional Road Race title in 1988

Steve Joughin

I might not be here today if it wasn't for the support of my wife Joanne and my sons, Ben and Tom. I put them through a lot when I was drinking and I wouldn't have overcome my problem without them.

I would also like to thank my mum and dad for all that they have done for me and for helping their tearaway son to realise his dreams of being a pro cycling champion and making them proud.

There are many cyclists that I've been lucky enough to race with and against, but particular thanks go to my old mates Eddie Kewley and Sid Barras, Brian Rourke, Ron Killey and Mike Kelly, who gave up a lot of their free time to ride motorbikes so I could do motor-paced training in the Isle of Man. Thanks to Geoff Quine for talking me into my first race, Frank Daniels, who was also a huge help when I needed to get to big races in the UK and often picked me up off the boat from the Isle of Man, and Richard Smith of Vitesse sportswear, for his support and faith in me.

Jack and Nora Fletcher became good friends and Jack's backing of Manchester Wheelers provided me with a stepping stone into the pro ranks for which I will always be grateful. Thanks also to Dianne and Peter Nowell for putting me up when I left the Island.

The nurses and staff at the Edward Myers Centre who helped me overcome my drink problem also have my sincerest thanks.

There are many more I could mention here who have helped me during my career, and afterwards, but I hope most are mentioned in this book and that they know how grateful I am for their friendship and support.

Thanks for the ride.

One day at a time.

Richard Allen

Firstly, I'd like to thank Steve for giving me the opportunity to write this book and for the hours of fun I've had reminiscing about that golden age of British cycling which I enjoyed as a spectator. It's been a pleasure to hear Steve tell some of the stories about what went on behind the scenes at races I used to watch on TV, at the roadside, or read about in magazines. I hope that this book does him, his career and his life, the justice it deserves.

John and Emma Quirk of Nemesis Publishing have done a wonderful job designing and producing this book. I'd also like to thank all those who have contributed their stories about Steve and helped me with research – most notably Peter Whitfield for access to interviews he conducted with Steve and also to Mike Doyle, Phil Liggett, Allan Peiper, Sid Barras, Isle of Man cycling performance director Gary Hinds and Manx International Week organiser Mike O'Hare.

Thanks also to Isle of Man Newspapers' sports editor John Watterson and former Isle of Man Newspapers' editor Lionel Cowin.

A big thank you to photographer Paul J Wright for allowing use of his superb archive of pictures. The cover photo is by Graham Watson who is for me, and many other admirers of his work, the best cycling photographer of them all. Thanks to Graham for allowing us to use his shot of Steve winning the Birmingham stage of the Kellogg's Tour of Britain. Alan Rushton, the director of the Kellogg's Tour, was also kind enough to give his approval to use the photo and kind enough to say that he gave that approval with pleasure and in respect to Steve in for his contribution to British cycling all those years ago.

On a personal note, thanks to my mum and dad for putting up with my obsession with cycling before I flew the nest.

Last but not least, the biggest thank you of all goes to Eileen, the love of my life. You are my inspiration. Thank you for encouraging me to write this book.

STEVE JOUGHIN

FACTFILE

Celebrating victory in the Merseyside Junior Championship in 1977, complete with Dennis the Menace haircut

JUNIOR

1975
1st Isle of Man Schoolboy Championship

1976
1st Mersey Division Junior Road Race Championship

1977
1st British Junior Road Race Championship
1st Pete Buckley British Junior Road Race Series
1st Mersey Division Junior Road Race Championship

Represented Great Britain at World Junior Road Race, Austria

Leading Mark Bell in the Douglas Kermesse, June 1981

SENIOR AMATEUR

1978
1st Tour of Ireland prologue time-trial

Represented Isle of Man at Commonwealth Games, Edmonton

1979
1st Manx International
Winner Tour of Armagh
King of the Mountains winner, Tour of Norway

1980
1st in season-long Pernod Trophy standings
1st GP of Essex
Stage win in Sealink International
1st Stage London to Glasgow Pro-Am 80
King of the Mountains winner, Tour of Ireland

1981
Stage win in Milk Race (Stage 1: Brighton to Bournemouth)
1st Tour of the Peak
1st GP Champion Supermarche, France
2nd in prologue, Ruben Grenatier Breton, France

Represented Great Britain at World Amateur Road Race, Czechoslovakia

In cyclo-cross action in Runcorn, 1989

1982
1st in season-long Raleigh Trophy standings
1st Tour of the Cotswolds
1st Essex Trophy
1st GP of Essex
1st Archer GP
1st Lancaster GP Pro-Am
1st GP of Vanquers
Stage win in Sealink International

Represented Great Britain at World Amateur Road Race, Goodwood, England

Represented Isle of Man at Commonwealth Games, Brisbane

1989 Milk Race stage winner in Liverpool

PROFESSIONAL

1983
Represented Great Britain at World Pro Road Race, Zurich

1984
1st British Pro Road Race Championship, Isle of Man)
1st Cleveland GP
Points Race Winner Tour of Ireland
1st in British Pro Rankings

1986
Two stage wins in Milk Race (Stage 1: Birmingham to Blackpool and Stage 12: London circuit)
Winner Michelin GP Series
1st in British pro rankings

1987
Stage win Kellogg's Tour of Britain (Stage 3: Manchester to Birmingham)

1988
1st British Pro Road Race Championship, Newport
1st in season-long Star Trophy standings

1989
Stage win Milke Race (Stage 6: Barnsley to Liverpool)

Team time-trial stage of 1989 Milk Race with Percy Bilton

CLUBS AND PRO TEAMS

Amateur
1973 to 1979 - Manx Road Club
1980 to 1982 - Manchester Wheelers/Trumann's Steel

Professional
1983 to 1986 - Moducel
1987 - Percy Bilton
1988 - Ever Ready
1989 - Percy Bilton
1990 - Percy's Direct Discounts
1991 - KGC Carpets